25   W 3103

LAST WILL AND TESTAMENT

LAST WILL AND TESTAMENT

WILLS, ANCIENT AND MODERN

FRANK THOMAS

DAVID & CHARLES

Newton Abbot

ISBN 0 7153 5978 X

Set in 11 on 13 point Plantin
and printed in Great Britain
by W. J. Holman Limited Dawlish
for David & Charles (Publishers) Limited
South Devon House Newton Abbot Devon

CONTENTS

ONE

INTRODUCTION

Wills have no pattern. They can be long or short, scrawled on an old envelope or prepared by legions of lawyers. They can be businesslike, eccentric, charitable. They can express love or hate, frivolity or reverence. They come in all shapes and sizes. All that is certain is that they try and tell the survivors what the testator wants to be done with his property.

Originally the word 'will' applied to real estate and 'testament' to personal estate, but the word 'will' is now taken to cover both.

Wills go back a long way into history: Sir Flinders Petrie discovered them while excavating Egyptian tombs over 4,500 years old. They are mentioned in the Bible, obliquely: Jacob left Joseph one portion more than his brothers; and the prophet Isaiah told King Hezekiah: 'Thus saith the Lord, Set thine house in order'. As the King was ill at the time, it was as good as suggesting he made a will. Most men and women are not prepared to leave this world without disposing of their property, and the worldly view is that such dispositions save the heir trouble; those who die intestate, however, may unconsciously feel that it is illogical to worry about what happens when one is dead, for 'we brought nothing into this world and it is certain we can take nothing out'. Magna Carta treated intestacy sensibly:

If a free man dies intestate, his movable goods are to be distributed by his next of kin and friends under the supervision of the Church. The rights of his debtors are to be preserved.

In thirteenth-century England it was impossible for a testator to will his lands, for his heir succeeded to them automatically; and by the fifteenth century his widow was entitled to a dower of a third of her husband's land. In the early days the wife was also entitled to a third of her husband's chattels, and may even, in some parts of England, have been allowed to will that portion, though generally she owned nothing in her lifetime. After her death, however, her lands would go to her heirs, which were usually but not always her husband's also.

The villein could make a will, but his lord could interfere before probate was granted, as his villein's goods were looked on as his.

Custom over a large part of the country laid down that a man's wife and children were entitled to two-thirds of his effects, so he could only leave a third elsewhere; but the law varied throughout the country and by the early eighteenth century, and much earlier in some parts, a man could dispose of his property as he wished. The Wills Act of 1540 allowed the free disposition of freehold land, and the Wills Act of 1837 confirmed (1) that a man might dispose of all he had by will; (2) that the will must be in writing; and (3) that witnesses must not benefit under it. Various acts followed for men in the armed forces, giving them rights like civilians. Through the centuries the law changed from allowing a man to will only about a third of his property to giving him the right to dispose of it all as he wished.

This right was checked by The Inheritance (Family Provision) Act, 1938, which laid down that a surviving widow or widower, unmarried daughter, disabled daughter, infant son (adopted or not), or child in the womb, should not be left penniless. Now, if the Court of Probate thinks insufficient provision has been allowed for their maintenance, it can revise a will accordingly.

Documents such as wills presuppose machinery for carrying them out: executors have to be appointed and wills have to be registered and proved or probated at certain offices set up for the purpose. The ancient Greeks deposited their wills at a public office, and they were signed and sealed in the presence of a magistrate. Solon is said to have inaugurated this practice, as he is said to have originated so many others, in Athens in the sixth century BC. The Romans pierced their wills, tying them with ribbon and adding their seals—a method established in the time of Nero (54-69 AD) to prevent forgery. Inside, the first page, or left-hand tablet, carried the names of the principal heirs and the opposite right-hand page the names of the legatees. Wills were first regulated in Rome as long ago as 450 BC. Anglo-Saxon wills were unusual in that the legatee had a copy as well as the testator.

A difficulty of rich testators in medieval days was in ensuring that their wills were carried out, and there are several wills in Chapter 4 showing that this was frequently accomplished by a disguised bribe in the form of a legacy to a king or some lesser potentate. One of the earliest examples of such bribery was the will of the Celtic king of the Iceni, Prasutagus, who died during the reign of the Emperor Nero. Prasutagus tried to make sure that his wife and children would inherit by making a large legacy to the Emperor, but as soon as he was dead the Romans took over the Iceni lands in East Anglia and ousted the queen and her children. The queen's name was Boudicca, and before she was killed herself she had led a revolt which came little short of destroying Roman rule in Britain.

During the Middle Ages the royal courts, which operated the common law, gradually turned over the administration of wills to the ecclesiastical courts. In England, up to 1858, most wills were probated in ecclesiastical courts, of which the most prominent was the Prerogative Court of Canterbury, though there were 372 altogether in England and Wales. But under the Court of Probate Act 1857 all ecclesiastical jurisdiction over wills was abolished. The number of courts was reduced to forty-one and from that date every will probated had to be filed, at least in copy, with the Principal Registry of the Court of Probate, Somerset House, London.

One of the problems for heirs and executors is finding wills after the testator's death. Sometimes they cannot be found at all, as with Lord St Leonards' (see p115). The will of another nobleman, Lord Hailes, who died in 1792, was found behind the panelling of a wall; in *Pickwick Papers* Tony Weller found his wife's will in a teapot; another will was found in a clock. The framers of the 1857 Act thought of this possibility and arranged that wills could be left at the Principal Probate Registry at Somerset House, where they would remain sealed until the testator's death; but this service has hardly ever been used, probably because once you have lodged your will with Somerset House, you cannot get it back and alter it if you wish, but have to make a new will instead. So wills are still left lying about in drawers mixed up with letters, in suitcases, or on top of the wardrobe in Aunt Mary's room.

The shortest will of all is supposed to be 'All for Mother', written on an old envelope. It says everything that is necessary: the amount of the estate—'all'—and the name of the legatee—'Mother'. One of the next shortest is positively wordy in comparison: 'Mrs —— to have all when I die'.

A will did not have to be written: it could be spoken, as long as there were witnesses to swear to it. This book contains several oral or noncupative wills.

Medieval wills and wills dated as late as the eighteenth century generally have a religious preamble, beginning 'In the Name of God, Amen', and continuing in a fairly standard fashion to state that the testator leaves his soul to the mercy and love of God and his body to be buried—and then he states where. Not everyone chose some cathedral, abbey or church; some wished to be buried at sea or have their ashes scattered on the water. Bernard Shaw asked for his ashes to be scattered over his garden, saying he preferred the garden to the cloister; and another country-lover, Thomas Hollis of Dorset, asked to be buried 10ft deep on his farm and the surface ploughed over so that no one should know where he lay. On the other hand, Emerald, Lady Cunard, who died in 1948, was such a confirmed Londoner that her friends scattered her ashes in Grosvenor Square. Robert Louis Stevenson asked to be buried on top of a Samoan mountain, where he still lies, and Thomas Jefferson near the crest of Monticello, Virginia. Cecil Rhodes, who died in 1902, said in his will: 'I admire the grandeur and loneliness of the Matoppos in Rhodesia and therefore I desire to be buried in the Matoppos on the hill which I used to visit and which I called the "View of the World" . . .'.

Lord Camelford, a well known duellist, wished to be buried in Switzerland by the lake at Lampierre, under a tree, which he directed should be dug up and then replaced over his coffin. Sir Charles Hastings asked to be buried somewhere where acorns could be planted over his body, which he hoped would 'nourish some good English oaks'. Lady Truro was buried under the lawn of her house 'Falconhurst' on Shooters Hill, London. Godfrey Winn, the writer who died in 1971 aged sixty-two, asked for his ashes to be scattered over the 'rich red Cotswold earth which has so many childhood memories for me', which was done, as he had asked, by aeroplane. 'England has been very good to me, and I am proud that I was born under the British flag and have lived my life on English soil', he wrote.

Gilbert White of Selborne, the famous naturalist, made the following request in his will:

And lastly to close all I do desire that I may be buried in the

11

Parish Church of Selborne aforesaid in as plain and private a
way as possible, without any pall bearers or parade, and that
six honest day-labouring men (respect being had to such as
have bred up large families) may bear me to my grave, to
whom I appoint the sum of ten shillings each for their trouble.

The request for a plain funeral, without mourning or
flowers, has been common enough over the years, and one
Frenchman even specified a pauper's funeral.

Testators have had fears throughout the ages which they
have expressed in their wills. One is the fear of being buried
alive. Indeed, there used to be a Society for the Prevention of
Premature Burials. Testators have asked the heirs to ensure
they were really dead by cutting off one of their fingers, or
even their heads, by piercing their hearts, or cremating them.
Others have requested that they remain unburied for a period
after their deaths (John of Gaunt specified forty days) in case
they recover. There is a story of a woman who was buried
with a ring on her finger and on the night after her burial her
butler came to her family vault to steal it. It was rather tight
and, as he was trying to remove it, she woke up! The butler
fled and she made her way back to her house in her grave
clothes, and lived happily for many more years.

Another source of trial for testators is the trustworthiness of
their executors. An attempt was made to ensure this in the
Statute of Distribution of 1670. It has been said, if one is
charitably inclined, that it is better to distribute what one has
to leave in one's lifetime than rely on one's heirs to do it. There
is an old proverb which says, 'Three executors make three
thieves' and a cynical poem in an old volume called Weever's
Funeral Monuments about those left behind:

> Man, thee behoveth of to have this in mind,
> That thow geveth wyth thin hond, that sall thow fynd.
> For widowes be sloful, and chyldren beth unkynd,
> Executors beth covetos, and kep al they fynd.

If eny body ask wher the deddys goodys becam,
They answer
So god help me and Halidam, he died a poor man.

Sometimes wills are ineffective because there is insufficient left for the bequests to be carried out. One testator left a bequest to build a hospital to 'maintain ancient maids', but the amount left was so small that Dr Johnson recommended that the word 'maintain' should be replaced by the word 'starve'.

Sometimes wills fail also because the bequests are against the law. There is no way in law of enforcing the dead man's wishes for the disposal of his body, except for anatomical pur·· poses; bequests of money whose interest is to be spent on keeping up a grave are not allowable; and since 1835 gifts to priests to say prayers or masses for one's soul or for the souls of others have been termed 'a superstitious trust' and are void. So there can now be no more of those splendid medieval wills of great lords or ladies specifying 'ten thousand masses to be said for my soul and for the souls of all Christians in the fourteen days following my death'. Why the law interfered in this matter, which surely cannot concern it, is beyond understanding.

Possibly the greatest fear among testators, however, is that they will not be remembered; and so, many of them have left instructions for certain deeds to be performed or certain charitable distributions to be made yearly in order that their names will live on. The legacy of marriage portions to young women who lacked them was common in the Middle Ages and this custom continued to the eighteenth century in the will of Richard Sumption in 1775, who left £1,000 worth of 3 per cent consols whose income was to be distributed at £10 a time to poor young women of Wilton in Wiltshire.

Testators are entitled to their whims and eccentricities before setting out on an unknown journey. Vanity, too, is excusable. Mrs Anna Oldfield, an actress who was buried in

13

Westminster Abbey in 1730, was very vain of her appearance. She was called Miss Nancy, from which incidentally we get the word 'nancies' for effeminate persons. In her will she was careful to order that she should be buried in her best gown, wearing her finest lace, and looking her best. Alexander Pope quotes her as remarking to her maid:

> One would not sure be frightful when one's dead,
> And—Betty—give this cheek a little red.

Finally, two books on wills, the first by Henry Swinburne in 1677 and the second by a 'Gentleman of the Law' in 1744, make the following observation in almost the same words:

> He that is overcome with Liquor, during the time of his Drunkenness is compared to a Madman, and therefore if he make his testament at that time, it is void in law; which is to be understood when he is so excessive drunk that he is utterly deprived of the Use of Reason and Understanding; otherwise if he be not quite spent, although his understanding be obscured, and his Memory troubled, yet he may make his Testament in that Case.

A breathalyser might have been useful.

TWO

ROYALTY

Few men have been able, like William the Conqueror, to leave a country to their *second* sons. Normandy belonged to William's eldest son, Robert, who became duke by inheritance, but England was a prize of war and the Conqueror could leave it to whom he wished. So he left it to William Rufus, who reigned as William II. So goes the story, but in fact William Rufus took England because he was there and Robert was in Normandy at the time.

William the Conqueror dictated his will in Rouen, leaving large sums to the clergy of Mantes, whose town he had burnt. Everything was done precisely—the Conqueror dictating what sums were to be distributed and who was to receive them, and his secretaries noting it all down. His third son, later Henry I, was given £5,000 in silver. Few men have left their sons better provided for. The great king died quietly, and tombs and monuments were raised to him in Normandy; though the iconoclastic spirit of the Huguenots in the sixteenth century destroyed them all.

William Rufus (1087-1100) died intestate. His body was found pierced by an arrow (he was probably murdered) in the New Forest, one of the hunting grounds of the Norman kings. His tomb in Winchester Cathedral was destroyed in the Civil War; a ring set with rubies, said to be worth £500, and a small

15

silver chalice were supposed to have been taken from it.

William the Conqueror's third son, Henry I (1100-35), succeeded to the English throne, as his elder brother Robert was still making his way home from the First Crusade. In 1105, Henry defeated Robert at Tenchebray in Normandy, largely with English forces (as distinct from Anglo-Norman), and thus added the dukedom of Normandy to England. His son William died in the wreck of the famous White Ship in 1120 and he made his heir his daughter Matilda, who had married the Count of Anjou. Henry's will gave his natural son Robert, Earl of Gloucester, who was with him when he died, £6,000 from his treasury at Falaise in Normandy to distribute to his followers and soldiers; and it directed that his body should be buried in Reading Abbey, which he had founded. He died at St Denys, in the Castle and Forest of Lions, in Normandy on 4 December 1135. No memorials now remain, the Huguenots having destroyed them, as they did those of his father.

Henry's daughter Matilda was not allowed to succeed him, the idea that a queen might rule in her own right being unacceptable to the baronage in twelfth-century England, and Stephen, a grandson of the Conqueror, was chosen. He left no will after a troubled reign. He died on 25 October 1154 and was buried at Feversham Abbey with his queen. Their bodies were torn from their graves at the time of the dissolution of the monasteries in the sixteenth century, for the sake of the lead in their coffins.

Stephen was succeeded by Henry II (1135-89), the first of the Angevin or Plantagenet kings, son of Henry I's daughter Matilda and Geoffrey, Count of Anjou. The story of Henry's reign is well know—his legal reforms, his quarrel with Becket, and his marriage to Eleanor of Aquitaine, which added so much to his French possessions that he ruled more of France than the French king—and he died before the altar of the church at Chinon on 6 July 1189, and was buried at Fontevrault in Anjou.

In his will Henry greets his sons and all the important men in his kingdom and orders that 5,000 marks of silver be distributed to the religious houses in England by the Archbishop of Canterbury and other bishops, and 1,000 marks of silver among the religious houses of Anjou. He leaves 300 marks of gold, 100 marks of gold and another 100 marks of gold to be given towards the marriages of poor and free women of England, Normandy and Anjou respectively. However, he had probably distributed all his bequests himself in 1182, thus fulfilling the first rule of a charitable testator—do it yourself. In his will he calls on his sons to honour these bequests, and on the archbishops and bishops to excommunicate anyone who interferes with them. He concludes by saying that the pope has confirmed the distribution on pain of anathema.

Henry's will also appears in verse in Peter Langtoft's *Rhyming Chronicle*. In the preamble to the poem Henry has to go to France, wondering whether the French want war or not and feeling his age:

He sauh wele bi signe, he drough [drew] fast tille elde [old age],
Long myght he not regne, ne on his lif belde [build].

Then comes a list of bequests:

Sex thousand marke tille Acres [Jerusalem] did he send,
Ageyn his comyng thidere, bi marchandz so he wend [thought].

Henry had lent 50,000 marks to certain poor abbeys so these are not listed. The rhyme goes on:

To Waltham ged the Kyng, his testament to make,
And thus quathe [bequeathed] he his thing, for his soule sake.
To temples [the Templars] in Acres he quathe five thousand
  marke
And five thousand to the hospitale [the Hospitallers] for they
  were in karke [charge].
To the folk that duelled, Acres for to fend [defend]
Other five thousand marke he gaf them to spende.
Tille other houses of the cuntre [Jerusalem] five thousand
  marke he gaf.

17

B

The mark was money of account, like our former guinea, and worth 13s 4d. The Kingdom of Jerusalem, which had been established after the successful First Crusade, 1096-9, in which Robert, Duke of Normandy, Henry's great-uncle, had taken part, was now just a fragment of a country, the city of Jerusalem having been recaptured by Saladin in 1187. The Christian kings of the West, however, had not given up the struggle and Richard, Henry's son and successor, spent the first three years of his reign crusading, though most of that time was spent getting to the Holy Land, and his father was anxious, if the *Chronicle* can be trusted, to further this work.

Then follow bequests to hermits, lepers, nuns, religious houses, and dowries to poor women of gentle birth in England and Anjou. He was very generous to the nuns of Fontevrault:

To them of Founz Eberard, there his body lis,
He gaf two thousand mark, tho ladies of pris [of rank or fortune].

Altogether Henry donated 45,000 marks for religious or charitable purposes, though his will was probably a form of accounting for bequests he had already distributed. It finishes:

Whan the kyng Henry had mad his testament,
He dight his oste [host] redy, and to Parys went.

His successor Richard I (1189-99) was struck by an arrow while besieging the castle of Chaluz in France and died at Gizors on 6 April 1199, pardoning the archer who had shot the arrow, though his men did not. He ordered his castle and three-quarters of his treasure to be delivered to his brother and successor, John, and the remaining quarter to his nephew Otto IV, Emperor of Germany, son of his sister Maud, who had married Henry V, the Lion, Duke of Saxony and Bavaria. He willed that his brains, his blood and his entrails should be buried at Charrou (Chaluz), his heart at Rouen, and his body at Fontevrault at the foot of his father; the requests were carried out as far as his heart and body were concerned.

18

The orders for the disposition of his remains were singular. He was an Angevin and Count of Anjou, and presumably that was the reason he wished to be buried at Fontevrault in Anjou; and as he was Duke of Normandy he wished his heart to be buried there, in the Norman capital. Anjou and Normandy in the twelfth century were generally suspicious of each other, like England and Scotland, and the Angevins were never really accepted as Norman rulers. So perhaps Richard's desire for his heart to be buried in Rouen was more than an assertion that he was their duke; maybe he was trying to heal the breach in his French possessions.

His successor John, however, soon lost those possessions. He died on 16 October 1216 and was buried in Worcester Cathedral. He made his will in the year he died.

The wills of the next half dozen kings can be dealt with quickly. John's son, Henry III, had a long reign (1216-72) and a troubled one. He made his will in 1253 at Southwick, Hants, when on his way to aid his Gascon subjects; at Southwick he stayed at the Priory of the Black Canons, where in the next century Henry VI and Margaret of Anjou were married, and willed he be buried at Westminster in the 'Church of the Blessed Edward' (Westminster Abbey).

He died on 16 November 1272 while his successor, Edward I, was crusading at Acre, where he made his will. It was a businesslike document dealing with the succession in case he and his father died before his children came of age. Edward died on 7 July 1307 at Burgh-upon-Sands while leading his army against the Scots, and Froissart records the famous story that Edward ordered that his bones should be carried in any future invasion at the head of the English troops to ensure victory; but apparently he did not add this provision to the will he had made thirty-five years before his death. He was buried in Westminster Abbey at the head of his father.

His son, Edward II, was murdered on 25 January 1327, and

his grandson Edward III (1327-77) died at his manor of Shene at Richmond in Surrey almost fifty years later, on 21 January 1377. Edward III left his grandson and heir, Richard II, a bed marked with the arms of France and England, perhaps symbolic of the fact that the first part of the Hundred Years' War, which ended with the Treaty of Bretigny in 1361, left England and France in very much the same position as when the war had begun.

Neither Richard II nor Henry IV left wills of particular interest. Richard was deposed by Henry on 4 September 1399 and soon afterwards murdered. He was first buried at Abbots Langley, Herts, but moved to Westminster Abbey by the second Lancastrian king, Henry V (1413-22). Henry IV made his will in 1408; he asked to be buried in Canterbury Cathedral and was.

Henry V made one will in 1417 as he was about 'to passe in to ye partes of France, to recover by help of God, my rightes yere to me longyng'. He had pretty well recovered his 'rightes' at the Battle of Agincourt in 1415. However, as this will was made three years before his marriage to Catherine of France, his heirs were his brothers—the Duke of Bedford, and if he were dead, the Duke of Gloucester—and not his son. Henry died two years later, in 1422, leaving the nine-month-old Henry VI as king.

Henry VI's reign was compounded of failing English fortunes in France, and, from 1450, the troubles of the Wars of the Roses. Henry was no warrior, and may have inherited the mental instability of his French grandfather. Probably the only way to have controlled the turbulent nobles of England in the fifteenth century would have been to set them, like the Vikings of old, to plunder foreign countries; but in France, the French, under Joan of Arc, were victorious, so the English were left to fight among themselves. Henry's reign lasted until 1461, with a brief return in 1471, and he was then murdered in the Tower of London by the victorious Yorkists; he was a cipher in politics and war, but as a founder of Eton and King's College, Cambridge, he has his claim to fame.

Much was done during his lifetime, but his will also includes elaborate instructions for the two foundations. Living at Windsor, he was quite close to the The King's College of Our Lady of Eton, and he built the chapel there. He associated the school with King's College, Cambridge, to which scholars were to go to finish their education. King's College chapel corresponds to Henry's designs. He was buried in St George's chapel, Windsor, though his body may have been later moved to Westminster by Henry VII.

Edward IV, Henry's Yorkist successor, despite his rakish private life, was a highly efficient monarch. Edward's brother, Richard III, whose name has never quite recovered from its treatment in Shakespeare's play, succeeded him as king. Edward IV's will was registered at Lambeth, though it may have been destroyed by Richard III. Edward IV's queen, Elizabeth, sank into insignificance during the reigns of his two successors, Richard III (1483-5) and Henry VII (1485-1509). She completed the foundation of Queen's College, Cambridge, however, which had been begun by Henry VI's queen, Margaret. On his succession Henry VII seized her possessions and she retired to Bermondsey Abbey, a Cluniac foundation of William Rufus. Her family of Woodville had been considered parvenu even in Edward IV's time. She died at Bermondsey and was buried as she requested near Edward IV at Windsor. Her will is dated 10 April 1492 and shows how poor she was, though her daughter Elizabeth was Henry VII's queen:

> It'm, where I have no wordely goods to do the Queen's Grace, my derest doughter, a pleaser with, nether to reward any of my children, according to my hart and mynde, I besech Almyghty Gode to blisse her Grace, with all her noble issue, and with as good hart and mynde as is to me possible, I geve her Grace my blessing, and all the forsaide my children.

Henry VII, who became king, and the first of the Tudor monarchs, by defeating Richard III at Bosworth Field in 1485, ostensibly represented the House of Lancaster, but really represented only himself. His father Edmund Tudor, Earl of Richmond, and Henry VI had been half-brothers, having had the same mother, Catherine of France, who had married Owen Tudor after the death of Henry V; and on his own mother's side Henry was a great-great-grandson of John of Gaunt. Most of those with better claims to the throne belonged to the defeated House of York.

Like William the Conqueror, Henry established his own line. He married the Yorkist heiress Elizabeth, Edward IV's daughter; so his son, Henry VIII, had a better claim to the throne, through the House of York, than he did. But, also like William the Conqueror, there was no doubt that he was king, as he makes clear in his will: he wants an image for his tomb made 'in timber, covered and wrought with plate of fine gold, in manner of an armed man and upon the same armour a coat-armour of our arms of England and France enamelled, with a sword and spurs accordingly and the said image to kneel upon a table of silver and gilt, and holding betwixt his hands the crown which it pleased God to give us with the victory over our enemy at our first field'.

Henry appoints a commission in his will to settle any man's complaint against his having taken 'any goods or lands which of right ought to appertain to him'. He left the Crown's finances in a very healthy state when he died in 1509. He had, in fact, extorted great sums from his nobles, completing their subjugation to the royal will that had been begun by Edward IV. One imagines the commission had very few sittings.

He also allocated money to the work on King's College, Cambridge, begun by Henry VI, whom he calls his uncle, and proposes to transfer Henry's body from Windsor to Westminster and inter it in the Henry VII chapel. He also desires to be buried in Westminster himself; and he wishes his 'great piece of the Holy Cross' to be placed in the grate of his tomb, and also 'the precious relic of one of the legs of St. George, set in silver, parcel gilt'. The first relic came from the Island of Scio in Greece and was 'set in gold and garnished with pearls and precious stones'; and the second was presented to Henry by the Cardinal of Amboys on behalf of Louis XII of France. Henry's will is dated 31 March 1509 and he died a few months later.

Henry VIII's will is enormously long, between 6,000 and 7,000 words, and is dated 30 December 1546. He died on 28 January 1547 and is buried at Windsor. It has a long religious preamble. Then he makes arrangements for the burial of his 'cadaver', saying that were it not for the

> dignitie which God hath called us unto and that we wold not be noted an infringer of honest worldlie policies and customs when they be not contrary to Godde's laws, we would be contented to have it buried in any place accustomed for Christian folke, were it never so vile. . . Nevertheless, because we would be lothe in the reputation of the people to do injurie to the dignitie which we unworthilie are called unto . . . our last will and testament do will and ordayne that our bodye be buried and interred in the queyr of oure colledge of Wyndsore, midwaye betweene the Stalles and the high aulter . . . in whiche we will also that the bones and body of our true and loving wif queen Jane be put also.

This request seems to prove that Queen Jane Seymour, who died after giving birth to Edward VI, was Henry's favourite queen.

It is also ordered that 'the tombes and aulters of King Henry the Sixth and also of King Edwarde the fourth, our greate uncle and grandefather be made more princely in the same places where they now be at our charges'. He leaves a great deal to charity. He settles the succession on his son Edward VI, and, if he should die without heirs, on his elder daughter,

Mary, and then on Elizabeth, assuming Mary dies without heirs. But if any of them marry without the consent of the Council of the Realm, they lose their inheritance. If Elizabeth dies childless, Henry specifies that the crown is to go not to the heirs of his sister Margaret, who married James IV of Scotland, but to the heirs of his younger sister Mary, whose second marriage was to Charles Brandon, Duke of Suffolk. Lady Jane Grey was Mary's grand-daughter and reigned for nine days after the death of Edward VI under the protection of her father-in-law, the Duke of Northumberland.

The question did not arise, but Henry also wills that if his queen at the time of his death, Katherine Parr, had any children, they should inherit the throne before the Princesses Mary or Elizabeth. He also leaves Katherine £3,000 in plate, jewels etc, and £1,000 in cash 'with the enjoyment of her dowry and jointure'. Mary and Elizabeth receive £10,000 each towards their marriages, and £3,000 each per annum to support them. He appoints the Council that is to govern during Edward VI's minority, and makes bequests to all his courtiers.

A king, however powerful, cannot command events after his death; despite his wishes, the heir of his sister Margaret eventually came to the throne in the person of James I.

Henry had done more than anyone in his lifetime to destroy the power of the Catholic Church in England. His contemporary, Charles V, Holy Roman Emperor, added a codicil to his will exhorting his son, Philip II of Spain, to stamp out the heresy of Luther in his dominions. Henry's first wife, whom he had divorced, was Katharine of Aragon and the Emperor's aunt. After the divorce Henry treated her harshly and she hardly had the means to pay her servants. She died in 1536 and in her will beseeches Henry 'to let me have the goods which I do hold, as well in gold and silver as in other things, and also the same that is due to me in money for the time passed to the intent that I may pay my debts and recompense my servants . . .'. Henry, however, paid no attention to her cry of distress, and her burial was simple and sombre. Thomas Fuller reports: 'she was buried in the abbey-church of Peterborough, under a hearse of black say; probably by her own appointment, that she might be plain when dead, who neglected bravery of clothes when living'.

The young Edward VI, who died in 1553 at the age of fifteen, was persuaded on his deathbed to will the throne to Lady Jane Grey by her father-in-law, the Protector Northumberland. But Queen Jane reigned only nine days.

After the Welsh dynasty of the Tudors came the Scottish Stuarts, Dutch William, and the German Hanoverians. The will of George I (1714-27) was suppressed by his son George II (1727-60). It was handed to him by the Archbishop of Canterbury, he put it in his pocket, and that was the last anyone heard of it. George I had divorced his wife, and, as George II supported his mother, father and son were always at daggers drawn. It is said that George I's will bequeathed a legacy to his daughter, the Queen of Prussia, but it was never paid.

George IV, who came to the throne in 1820, wished to have his marriage to Queen Caroline dissolved by act of parliament, as he had left her and accused her of infidelity; but public opinion prevented this. Queen Caroline, in fact, died on 7 August 1821, having made her will on 5 August. On that day she had sent for the undertaker and been measured for the cedarwood coffin she wished to be buried in. She had also added a codicil to her will asking for the following plaque to be fixed to her coffin, the date of death to be added when it was known:

CAROLINE OF BRUNSWICK
Born 17th May, 1768
Died 7th August, 1821
Aged 54.
The Outraged Queen of England.

Naturally, the king was unlikely to allow such a plaque to be fixed, so the faithful members of her entourage waited until the arrival of her coffin at Colchester, where it was to be kept in a chapel overnight with a guard of honour, en route for Brunswick, where she was to be buried, and stole in and fixed the plate as she had asked. But in the morning the plate was discovered by the king's men in charge of the cortege, who were highly scandalised and removed it, substituting a plain plate and omitting her final denunciation of her husband.

When George IV made his own will he acknowledged that Mrs Fitzherbert was his wife and commanded the Duke of Wellington, who was then prime minister, to see that he was buried in the clothes he wore at his death and that nothing should be removed from his body. By this means, it is said, he contrived to be buried wearing a miniature of Mrs Fitzherbert. George IV had married Mrs Maria Anne Fitzherbert in her drawing room, when he was Prince of Wales, on 21 December 1785, but as the heir to the throne could not marry without the king's consent until he was twenty-five, and was forbidden to marry a Roman Catholic in any case, the marriage was invalid. He married Caroline of Brunswick ten years later, a marriage that was quite unsuccessful.

Royal wills today are proved but remain unopened, and the contents are not published.

THREE

LOVE AND HATE

Hate predominates, unfortunately, though sometimes in the milder form of scorn. Testators who love their families hardly bother to say so in their wills; it is taken for granted. Love, however, certainly motivated the will, made in 1528, of Thomas Trethurfe, a Cornish gentleman. The John Vyvyan mentioned was his son-in-law, husband of his daughter Elizabeth:

> Item, I will and bequeath all my tin-works, wheresoever they be . . . to Alice Christopher, the wife of William Christopher, during her life, according to my last will. . . Also I will that the Churches Store of St. Columb the Nether shall have the one halfe of my bote, with the half of my seynne net, and all things belonging to the same att Towne. And th'other half I give to Alice, the wife of the said William Christopher. And as for my goods within my doors and howse, first, I geve to John Vyvyan, my son, to the intent that he be good to see my will performed and fulfilled, and to helpe and ayde the forenamed Alice to have and to enjoy all such things as I doo will and entend hereafter to give her, for her great labor and paynes taken with me and my howse: first, a pott of silver, a salte of gold with a cover, a great brasen pott, a chitell, two fetherbedds, and two flock bedds. And all the residew of my goods and stuffe within my doors and howse I geve to Alice, the wife of the said William Christopher. Also I will that after my decease all my corne and cattell, as horses, kyne, oxen, etc. be

27

devided between my son, John Vivian, and Ales, the wife of
William Christopher. And to the entent that the said Ales may
have and enjoy all such things as I have given her, or do entend
to geve her, I do constitute and ordayne them too, my sonne,
John Vyvyan, and Ales, the wife of the said William Christopher, mine executors, to dispose the rest of my goods to the
pleasure of God, to the helthe of my sowle, and to the discharge of their conscience. And if my sonne, John Vyvyan, will
not ayde and helpe her to obtayne and enjoy the forsaid gifts
and bequests, I will that the forsaid Ales, the wife of the said
William Christopher, shalbe my sole and full executrix...

John Vyvyan agreed to act as executor and the will was proved
in the court of the Archdeacon of Cornwall on 26 October
1529. N. H. Nicolas in *Testamenta Vetusta* sums up Thomas
Trethurfe's will thus: 'It would perhaps be difficult to explain
the motives which induced the Testator to bequeath the chief
part of his property to Alice, the wife of William Christopher,
in a manner creditable either to his memory or her virtue'.

The next two entries show men's bitterness against their
wives. The first, from the will of Sir Robert Bevill, a courtier
to James I, shows a division in the family: 'Item: I give unto
my wife tenn shillings in respect she took her sonnes part
against me, and did anymate and comfort him afterwards'.
The second is from the will of William Pym of Woolavington,
Somerset, in 1608:

I give to Agnes, which I did a long time take for my wyfe—till
shee denied me to be her husband, all though we were marryd
with my friends' consent, her father, mother, and uncle at it;
and now she swareth she will neither love mee nor evyr be
perswaded to, by preechers, nor by any other, which hath
happened within these few yeres. And Toby Andrewes, the
beginner, which I did see with my own eyes when hee did
more than was fitting, and this by means of others their abet-
tors. I have lived a miserable life this six or seven yeres, and
now I leve the revenge to God—and tenn pounds to buy her a
gret horse, for I could not this manny yeres please her with one
gret enough.

This reads like the will of an old man with a young wife, though he does say that they have been married for a long time. Toby Andrewes, the 'beginner', may have been a young apprentice. Pym died in 1610 and the will was carried out.

The next will, in the form of a letter, is dated 1665, in the middle of the Dutch Wars, and is a pleasant change from the anger and bitterness we have just met:

> John Vincent (from abroad the *Unicorn* riding with the Fleet not far from Harwich April 12, 1665).
>
> Right Worshipful, I safely arrived in the Downs from the Straits the 22nd day of March last and got to London on Easter Eve, where I presented myself to the Dean of Westminster and other friends. But on Easter Monday I was engaged by Sir William Penn to go along with him to the Great Fleet under the command of his Royal Highness the Duke of York, the which I readily embraced... I am at present constituted chaplain aboard the *Unicorn*... Our fleet I can assure you is in a gallant posture, lying not far from Harwich, at all points ready for action. I freely refer myself to the goodness of my God, who hath preserved me hitherto in many dangers (viz) of battle, shipwrecks, fire and storms etc. And if I shall be taken out of the world my desires are ... that such moneys of mine as are in your worship's hands, or aught else due to me...be ... paid unto Alexander Vincent, the eldest son of my brother Ambrose Vincent... I wish all prosperity and happiness to yourself, Dr Allestry, and my friends at Christ Church, and remain your much obliged and true friend and servant John Vincent.

Samuel Pepys, who was at that time Clerk of the Acts and the mainstay of the Navy Office, wrote four days earlier, on 8 April, in his diary:

> It is thought they [the French ambassadors] come to get our King to joyne with the King of France, in helping him against Flanders, and they to do the like to us against Holland. We have lain a good while with a good fleete at Harwich. The Dutch not said yet to be out. We, as high as we make our

shew, I am sure, are unable to set out another small fleete, if
this should be worsted. Wherefore, God send us peace! I cry.

Sir William Penn was Comptroller of the Navy, and father
of the Quaker William Penn who founded the state of Penn-
sylvania. The Duke of York, who afterwards became James II,
has generally had a bad time in the history books, yet as Lord
High Admiral he did his best for the navy in those penurious
days, and Pepys had a high opinion of him. Pepys' fears that
if the fleet was beaten there was no money to 'set out another
small fleete' even, were unjustified, for the Duke of York won
a great victory over the Dutch on 3 June 1665.

Naval men seem more loving than landsmen, perhaps because their environment brought death nearer their conscious-
ness, or perhaps because they did not see so much of their
loved ones. John Wakring's will was in the form of a letter,
dated 23 November 1664 from the *Resolution*:

> Mistress Elizabeth, my kind love and respects . . . I have pre-
> sumed, hoping it will be acceptable, to acquaint you of the
> receival of your letter wherein I received much joy to hear of
> your welfare. I should think myself the happiest man alive if I
> could attain so much time as for to see you before my depar-
> ture, but since God has decreed it otherwise by reason of
> much business imposed on me, nevertheless I would have you
> accept of all that is mine as yours if God shall deal with me
> otherwise than I do expect. . . I am at the time Sir William
> Barkley's cook and am in very much respect on all sides, and
> hope, for all these wars, I shall see you in good estate if God
> permit.

This will was proved on 14 June 1665, so John Wakring may
have died in the sea battle with the Dutch on 3 June 1665,
previously mentioned. The *Resolution* is known to have been
heavily engaged, but Sir William Barkley must have moved to
another command, for her captain was Rear-Admiral Robert
Sansum, who was killed in the action.

From love to hate again we move to the will of Henry, Earl

of Stafford, who remained faithful to James II in 1688 and followed him into exile in France, where he married a daughter of the Duc de Grammont:

> To the worst of women, Claude Charlotte de Grammont, unfortunately my wife, guilty as she is of all crimes, I leave five-and-forty-brass halfpence, which will buy a pullet for her supper. A better gift than her father can make her; for I have known when, having not the money, neither had he the credit for such a purchase; he being the worst of men, and his wife the worst of women... Had I ever known their characters I had never married their daughter, and made myself unhappy.

The will of Robert Frampton of Woodley, Sonning, Berkshire, dated 18 December 1677, condemns his wife but makes some amends by leaving her a considerable sum of money:

> I do devise and bequeath to my wife Ann £1,000 to be paid her out of my personal estate, not being able to leave her any more by reason of her extravagancy in all things, embezzling the money given her for her apparel and leaving what she bought for that use upon the score, which I was forced to pay, and her running me into debt a good sum besides whereof she would never give any account. She hath also from time to time given her gossips a great part of what bought for herself, the children and necessaries for the house and of the provisions thereof to the huge increase of my expenses and great damage to my estate; yea, in all things she hath ever been a profuse, imperious and unkind wife unto me, and sundry times bound herself under a curse to ruin me if she could and necessitate the children to beg and starve.

Buying 'upon the score' is what we now should call 'charging to one's husband's account'. Mrs Frampton seems also to have had a number of hangers-on or 'gossips', who helped her spend her husband's money.

From anger to love, and the will of Richard Mathews, a servant of Spring Gardens, London, who died in October 1779, perhaps from a broken heart:

31

It is my further desire that 5s apiece may be given to the men as carries me to church, and it is my further desire to be buried in a decent manner and my body laid by a young woman who died at the Rev Mr. Allet's some time ago.

Love and affection permeate the will of Mary, the Dowager Countess de la Warr, which is in the form of a letter, dated 24 July 1783, to her son:

The silver cup given by your grandfather to my dear and most lamented son William Lord de la Warr I bequeath to you with my blessing, which no son was ever more entitled to receive from a fond mother than yourself; may it prove propitious to you, and that every affectionate attention shown to me may be returned to you by your children, that you may have the happiness and satisfaction of knowing how much comfort your behaviour administered to me who must long since have sunk under the weight of such repeated misfortunes, had they not been alleviated by the kindnesses of you and my dearest Georgiana.

She remembers her servants and continues:

My dear son, as I hourly feel my health decay, it reminds me how necessary it is to make a few memorandums, which, from the knowledge I have of the integrity of your heart, will (I am sensible) be as binding and as strictly adhered to as a will strictly drawn up with the greatest form... Poor Elizabeth Hutchinson's unwearied attentions to me and your sister Charlotte during all our sickness cannot be forgot by me. I desire she may have £30 and all my wearing apparel, and added to these the best of characters. The rest of my servants mourning and £10 each, having behaved very well in my service. *Adieu, jusqu'au revoir.*

One hopes that these bequests were attended to; considering the confidence expressed by the mother in the noble character of her son, they probably were.

This high standard cannot last. We now turn to Mr Swain of Southwark, who gave 'to John Abbot, and Mary his wife, 6d each, to buy for each of them a halter, for fear the sheriffs should not be provided'; and an early nineteenth-century husband who left his wife 500 guineas, not during her life but after her death, so 'that she may be buried suitably as my widow'!

John George of Lambeth, who died in June 1791, waxes eloquent on the subject of his wife's perversity:

> Seeing that I have had the misfortune to be married to the aforesaid Elizabeth, who, ever since our union, has tormented me in every possible way; that not content with making game of all my remonstrances, she has done all she could to render my life miserable; that Heaven seems to have sent her into the world solely to drive me out of it; that the strength of Samson, the genius of Homer, the prudence of Augustus, the skill of Pyrrhus, the patience of Job, the philosophy of Socrates, the subtlety of Hannibal, the vigilance of Hermogenes, would not suffice to subdue the perversity of her character; that no power on earth can change her, seeing we have lived apart during the last eight years, and that the only result has been the ruin of my son, whom she has corrupted and estranged from me; weighing maturely and seriously all these considerations, I have bequeathed, and I bequeath, to my said wife Elizabeth, the sum of one shilling.

What a stream of eloquence, and what anger and frustration must have caused it! And what was Elizabeth George's side of the story?

Another Englishman expressed his hate not just for one person but a whole race. He died on 17 March 1791, in what he considered was exile in Tipperary:

> I give and bequeath the annual sum of ten pounds, to be paid in perpetuity out of my estate, to the following purposes. It is my will and pleasure that this sum shall be spent in the purchase of a certain quantity of the liquor vulgarly called whisky, and it shall be publicly given out that a certain number of persons, Irish only, not to exceed twenty, who may choose to assemble in the cemetery in which I shall be interred, on the anniversary of my death, shall have the same distributed to them. Further, it is my desire that each shall receive it by half-

c

a-pint at a time till the whole is consumed, each being likewise provided with a stout oaken stick and a knife, and that they shall drink it all on the spot. Knowing what I know of the Irish character, my conviction is, that with these materials given, they will not fail to destroy each other, and when in the course of time the race comes to be exterminated, this neighbourhood at least may, perhaps, be colonised by civilised and respectable Englishmen.

The Marquis d'Aligre, an eccentric French nobleman of the nineteenth century, who used to dress shabbily, left much of his fortune to the poor. There are, however, three clauses in his will which express regard and scorn, the latter predominating:

> Art X—I leave 20,000 francs a-year to the *invalide* who, being on guard on the Pont des Arts in 1839, and judging from the shabbiness of my dress that I was in distress, paid for me the five centimes toll.
> Art XIV—I leave 200,000 francs a-year to the 'Phalansterians'; but they are only to receive this sum on the day on which they shall have transformed the ocean into orangeade, and gratified mankind with the appendage he needs to make him equal to the gibbon.
> Art XX—Finally, I leave to my relations oblivion; to my friends ingratitude; to God, my soul. As for my body, it belongs to my family vault.

The *invalide* was an old soldier, maybe disabled, and the Phalansterians were idealists who thought that one day, in the 'era of complete harmony', the sea would lose its salt and become like lemonade (or orangeade).

H. G. Wells, who died in 1946, expresses his love for his children in his will:

> ... and finally I want to put on record my loving recognition of the good and sane behaviour of all my offspring towards me and each other, and of the abundant content and happiness with which they have enriched my life, and I leave them my benediction.

CONDITIONAL WILLS

Some wills are loving enough, yet contain a hint of exasperation, and lay down conditions. Lord Chesterfield, famous for the crushing snub he received from Samuel Johnson, to whom he wished to extend his patronage when it was too late, left the bulk of his property to his godson Philip Stanhope (1773), but he was evidently doubtful about the young man's pastimes:

... in case my said godson Philip Stanhope shall at any time hereafter keep, or be concerned in the keeping of, any race-horse or race-horses, or pack or packs of hounds, or reside one night at Newmarket, that infamous seminary of iniquity and ill-manners during the course of the races there, or shall resort to the said races, or shall use in any one day at any game or bet whatsoever the sum of £500, then, and in any of the cases aforesaid, it is my express Will, that he my said Godson shall forfeit and pay out of my estate the sum of £5,000 to and for the use of the Dean and Chapter of Westminster, for every such offence or misdemeanour as is above specified, to be recovered by action for debt in any of his Majesty's Courts of Record at Westminster.

Walter Frampton, mayor of Bristol, who died on 6 December 1838, laid a condition on his wife (to whom he left a large property) which men, to do them credit, do not often make. He forbade her to remarry on pain of losing it all, and laid down that if she did her guilt would be blazoned abroad 'by making a triple proclamation of the same by sound of trumpet at the high Cross', presumably at Bristol.

The will of Sam Houston, who defeated the Mexicans and founded the independent state of Texas, is not exactly conditional but lays down some firm regulations for the education of his sons. He died in 1863, by which time Texas had become a state of the USA.

Third: My will is that my sons should receive solid and useful education, and that no portion of their time may be devoted to the study of abstract science. I greatly desire that they may possess a thorough knowledge of the English language, with a good knowledge of the Latin language. I also request that they be instructed in the knowledge of the Holy Scripture, and next to these that they may be rendered thorough in a knowledge of Geography and History. I wish my sons early taught an utter contempt for novels & light reading. In all that pertains to my sons I wish particular regard paid to their morals as well as to the character and morals of those with whom they may be associated or instructed.

This is almost the will of a Roman father.

Another father, this time in 1804, was—like fathers before and after—concerned with the way his daughter dressed. He was a Yorkshire rector, and left a considerable amount of property to her under two conditions: (1) she must not marry without the consent of the two executors, and (2) she must dress with greater propriety:

Seeing that my daughter Anne has not availed herself of my advice touching the objectionable practice of going about with her arms bare up to the elbows, my will is that, should she continue after my death in this violation of the modesty of her sex, all the goods, chattels, moneys, land, and other that I have devised to her for the maintenance of her future life shall pass to the oldest of the sons of my sister Caroline. Should anyone take exception to this my wish as being too severe, I answer that licence in dress in a woman is a mark of a depraved mind.

Testators frequently try to perform actions in their wills that they have never succeeded in performing while they were alive, and the rector seems a case in point.

Some conditional wills forbid marriage to persons of a particular religion, others oppose drink and gambling—one opposes moustaches. The conditional will of Stanislas Poltzmarz, dated 1835, however, was more in the nature of a practical joke, or 'succeeding by ordeal'. Poltzmarz lived in Pesth and bequeathed his fortune of 3 million florins to a notary called Lotz on condition that he sang in *Otello* and *La*

Sonnambula at La Scala, Milan. The testator had heard Lotz sing at a party and considered he had a fine tenor voice; so he concluded that the task was not beyond him. 'If therefore, I am right, he will thank me, and so will all *dilettanti*, for my acumen; if, on the other hand, he should fail, he may have money enough to compensate for the hisses he may incur'. At the time both Pesth, part of Budapest, and Milan were in the Austrian Empire, and the whole will smacks of that frivolous and ramshackle edifice. But one hopes Lotz was a success.

SERVANTS

Unless they are loved, servants are not usually mentioned in wills. Dr Johnson's Negro servant, Francis Barber, was indeed his main legatee (see p127); and others frequently receive a year's wages. Some wills, however, seem rather calculating, like the will of Nancy Greensill, a widow, of Brewood, Staffordshire, dated 4 January 1786. She left her servant Sarah Williams the following items:

> ... my old wearing apparel, my worst pair of stays, my old brown cotton gown, my black stuff gown, my light striped chintz gown, my black quilted petticoat, my bed gowns, my worst mourning cap, three plain muslin handkerchiefs, my common shoes, some thread stockings and my black bonnet.

Robert Dunant, a Swiss counsellor of State in Geneva, however, whose will is dated 12 August 1768, was much more generous, though perhaps he had more to leave:

> I give and bequeath to Elizabeth or Isabeau Rambosson my servant, if she be in my service at the time of my death the bed she lays on with all its furniture both inward and outward, three strikes of wheat with three good wheat sacks, twelve kitchen table cloths at her choice, thirty livres to buy her some necessaries, thirty livres in mourning ... in all three hundred livres in money, four pairs of sheets for the use of her bed, the aforesaid legacies free from the 10 per cent., and payable a month after my decease. The long, good and faithful

37

service of the aforesaid Isabeau ought to procure her moreover civility from my heirs.

In the Geneva of the time the death duty was evidently 10 per cent.

Some servants are 'characters', as was old Maman Conord. Her master died in 1868. He had been a former *deputé* (or MP), and was a dedicated legitimist (or supporter of the Bourbons) at a time when Napoleon III was emperor. He wanted to leave his fortune of 1,100,000 francs to the exiled legitimist heir, the Comte de Chambord, but he was afraid that this disposition would be disallowed by the courts. So he made Maman Conord his heir, instructing her to take his fortune to the comte on his death. She set off faithfully with the money, travelling third class to save expense, to Frohsdorf in Austria, where the comte was living.

The astonished comte received her and accepted the bequest, then asked how he could repay her for her efforts. She said all she wanted was to embrace him and then would be off, which she did and returned to Paris, where she continued working until she died at the age of eighty-five. The old lady had a poor sister, with five sons and daughters, who heard that the postman had delivered registered letters regularly to old Maman, whom nobody expected to leave much. A search in her rooms revealed 80,000 francs in gold and Maman Conord's will, which stated that the Comte de Chambord had insisted on paying her a yearly income of 6,000 francs which she did not want, and ordering that it should all be returned to him. This was too much for the sister to stomach, so she went to the comte and explained the matter, and was allowed to keep the money.

Independence could hardly be carried further than this.

ANIMALS

Animals are always loved in wills. Some testators make

provision for their pets to be destroyed after their deaths in case they grieve or are not looked after properly by their heirs. One tragic case occurred in May 1971, when two sisters, Edna and Joan Leech of Maldon, Essex, were killed in an air crash on their way to a holiday in Yugoslavia; they had specified in their wills that their collie dog Laddie, a faithful companion for fifteen years, should not long outlive his mistresses. In Shaw's *The Devil's Disciple*, Richard inherits Timothy Dudgeon's estate on condition that 'he shall be a good friend to my horse Jim'; and Richard promises that the horse shall live in clover.

Animals that are not pets are left just like other possessions. Richard Browne of Kent, in 1530, wished 'to be buried in the Church of Cowling in mydyll alley wher for I bequeath to the church a cow to be dryvyn to church with me at my beryall'. John Coward of Westpennard, Somerset, in his will dated 9 October 1590 and a codicil dated 9 January 1592, left to his brother Thomas 'my greate clocke nowe in my house goynge. To William Watkynnes my little clocke ... nowe to be emended'. In the codicil, he left to Mary Watkynnes 'my best baye amblinge mare'; and to his son Thomas Coward:

> my best geldinge yf he not taken for a heryott. And unto Edward Coward my sonne the other geldinge. If any of theise geldinges be taken for an heryot, then my will and intent is that by my overseers a choice be made of the fittest and best colte I have to make a geldinge when they ar in theire pryme at sommer. I give allso to William Watkynnes, gentleman (choice being first made for my sonne) one other colte to make hym a geldinge in the prime tyme in sommer, when they are best in shewe. Item, I give to Richard Siote, my guide, a good heiffer yerelinge, a fustian dublett, my best white frise jerkin, a payer of breches parte of the velvett being worn awaye with my sworde, and a payer of russett stockinges. Item, I give unto Elizabeth Kitchen the cloathe which she hathe in keepinge to make me a shirte.

A heriot was a payment to one's lord to make sure that the will was carried out.

Turning to pets, bequests have been made to parrots, goldfish, dogs, cats, horses, monkeys and others. Lord Chesterfield left a sum for the maintenance of his cat. In 1677, Madame Dupuis, a famous French harpist, made elaborate provision for her cats:

> Item: I desire my sister, Marie Bluteau, and my niece, Madame Calonge, to look to my cats. If both should survive me, thirty sous a-week must be laid out upon them, in order that they may live well.
>
> They are to be served daily, in a clean and proper manner, with two meals of meat soup, the same as we eat ourselves, but it is to be given to them separately in two soup-plates. The bread is not to be cut up into the soup, but must be broken into squares about the size of a nut, otherwise they will refuse to eat it. A ration of meat, finely minced, is to be added to it; the whole is then to be mildly seasoned, put into a clean pan, covered close, and carefully simmered before it is dished up. If only one cat should survive, half the sum mentioned will suffice.
>
> Nicole-Pigeon is to take charge of my two cats, and to be very careful of them. Madame Calonge is to visit them three times a week.

Jonathan Jackson of Columbus, Ohio, a nineteenth-century cat lover, left orders in his will for a cat's home to be built, with instructions how it was to be laid out: there were to be dormitories, a refectory, areas for conversation, grounds for exercise, gently sloping roofs for climbing, rat-holes for sport, an auditorium where the cats were to meet every day and listen to an accordion for one hour (that instrument was the nearest approximation he could think of to a cat's voice), and an infirmary. A surgeon and nurses were to be employed to look after the cats.

A Mr Berkeley, on the other hand, a Londoner, who died on 5 May 1805 in Knightsbridge, was a dog-lover, and left a pension of £25 to his four dogs. One of their forbears had accompanied him on a journey overseas and had saved his life when he had been attacked by brigands. He died with his four dogs round him, and gave orders that busts of each should be carved and fixed on the four corners of his grave.

A Mr Garland, who died in 1828, seems to have preferred his pets to his daughter:

> ... to my monkey, my dear and amusing Jacko, the sum of £10 sterling per annum, to be employed for his sole and exclusive use and benefit; to my faithful dog Shock, and my well-beloved cat Tibb, a pension of £5 sterling; and I desire that in the case of the death of either of the three, the lapsed pension shall pass to the other two, between whom it is to be equally divided. On the death of all three the sum appropriated to this purpose shall become the property of my daughter Gertrude, to whom I give this preference among my children, because of the large family she has and the difficulty she finds in bringing them up.

Another dog-lover was Sir James South, an astronomer who died in 1868. He left £30 a year to one of his maidservants to look after his favourite fox terrier Tiger.

Working horses in the nineteenth century had a great deal of trouble starting the carts they pulled because of the slippery road surfaces, which might be cobbles, asphalt, wood blocks, etc. Their plight occasioned Mrs Lisetta Rist, who died at Stratford, London, in the 1870s, to leave £1,500 to start a 'gravelling trust'. The interest was to be used to buy sand and gravel for spreading on certain roads in the City of London and the East End in slippery weather, and also for clearing away snow. The gravelling was to start in November and continue to the end of April, and to be spread on the roads by six-thirty or seven in the morning.

In his book *True Animal Stories*, E. R. Delderfield quotes the case of the cairn terrier Sherry, who must be the richest dog in England. His owner, Mrs Vera Rae of New Brighton in Cheshire, died in 1969 and left Sherry £33,000.

41

The amount received in legacies in 1970 by the Royal Society for the Prevention of Cruelty to Animals was something like £850,000. This amount is sometimes unfairly compared with that received by the similar society dealing with children, but it must be remembered that the State spends enormous sums on children's welfare, as do the local authorities.

FOUR

LORDS AND LADIES

The wills of noble lords and ladies are far more interesting than those of ordinary people, since they have more to leave. Several testators in the twelfth and thirteenth centuries, like Richard the Lionheart, willed not only their possessions but their hearts also. Robert, Earl of Mellent and Leicester, a crusader who died in 1118 at the Abbey of Preaux, where he was buried, ordered that his heart should be sent to the hospital at Brackley, where it was to be preserved in salt; Isabella, daughter of William Marshall, Earl of Pembroke, died at Berkhampstead in 1239, and ordered her heart to be sent to her brother, the Abbot of Tewkesbury, in a silver cup and buried before the high altar; and John Baliol, Lord of Barnard Castle and father of a later King of Scotland, who died in 1269, had his heart preserved by the desire of his widow and enclosed in an ivory casket chased with silver. The idea was that, though the body was buried and would return to the earth whence it came, the heart would remain in a favourite place or with a favourite person, still showing the love of the deceased.

Edward, the Black Prince, left lengthy instructions on how his tomb was to be prepared in Canterbury Cathedral. His will is dated the day before his death, and he must have spent most of that day preparing it. He had suffered from dysentery and died on 8 June 1376, leaving his ten-year-old son Richard as heir to the throne. The prince's father, Edward III, survived him for seven months, dying in January 1377. The prince disposed of four beds in his will: the first to his son Richard, which was the bed he had received from Edward III; the second, a silk bed, to Sir Roger de Clarendon, who was probably his natural son; the third to Sir Robert de Walsham, his confessor—a large bed of red camora (a rich stuff or silk) with the prince's arms embroidered at each corner, and the arms of Hereford; and the fourth to Monsieur Aleyne Cleyne—'our bed of camora embroidered with blue eagles'.

The Black Prince's wife, Joan, Princess of Wales, also left several beds in her will. Her best bed went to her son Richard II—it was a new bed of red velvet, embroidered with ostrich feathers of silver and heads of leopards of gold with boughs and leaves issuing from their mouths. Then, to Thomas, Earl of Kent, her son by an earlier marriage, a 'bed of red camak paied red and rayes of gold'; and finally to John Holland a bed of red camak.

Joan had been married first to Thomas Montacute, Earl of Salisbury, when she was sixteen, but the Pope allowed a divorce because the marriage had not been consummated; and she next married Sir Thomas Holland, KG, bringing him the earldom of Kent, for she was the daughter of Edmund of Woodstock, Earl of Kent and son of Edward I. Sir Thomas died in 1359, and in 1361 she married her cousin, the Black Prince. John Holland was her son by her second marriage and Richard II her son by her third. It was said she died of grief at Wallingford Castle in August 1385 because of Richard's resentment at John Holland's killing Lord Stafford in a fray. John Holland afterwards became Duke of Exeter.

Great heiresses of the day were often married several times, probably as the best way of looking after their lands; and they were generally buried with their first husband, as was Joan at

Stamford, her first husband being considered Sir Thomas Holland as her first marriage was not consummated.

Another son of Joan by Sir Thomas was his successor as Earl of Kent, also called Thomas (1350-97), who became Marshal of England, Constable of the Tower, and Governor of Carisbrooke Castle. His will is interesting because it is one of the first in English; before that Norman-French or Latin were commonly used.

Human problems and the perfidy of princes are occasionally touched on in the will of a soldier or statesman. In some wills, such as Charles Brandon's (p55), one sees that it is wise to make a large gift to the king to ensure that one's will is carried out, and in the will of Sir Walter Manny, a soldier and statesman of an earlier age, one sees how perhaps hope triumphs over experience, or how one may bequeath what one has not got. Sir Walter's will was made in 1371 and reads:

> Whereas the King [Edward III] oweth me an old debt of a thousand pounds, by bills of his wardrobe, I will that, if it can be obtained it shall be given to the Prior and Monks of the Charter-house.
>
> And whereas there is due to me from the Prince [the Black Prince] . . . the sum of c marks per annum, for my salary as Governor of Hardelagh Castle, I bequeath one half thereof to the said Prior . . . and the other half to the executors of my will.

The famous John of Gaunt, Duke of Lancaster and brother of the Black Prince, faced the same difficulty as Sir Walter Manny. He had been awarded a pension by the King of Castile and Leon for not pressing his claim to that throne in the right of his second wife Constance, daughter of Pedro the Cruel. Payment was evidently irregular, for in his will John left King Richard II a third part of the arrears of his pension if the king helped to recover them.

John of Gaunt's will is full of life, if one can say that about a will, and reads almost as if he had sat down and written it himself. He wills that he be buried in St Paul's Cathedral in London near the principal altar, beside his first wife Blanch, daughter and heiress of Henry, Duke of Lancaster, who brought him his title; and he insists that he is not to be buried for forty days after his death, and without cering or embalming. 'Cering' was wrapping up the body in a waxed cerecloth. The forty days' delay may have been due to a horror of being buried alive.

He orders all his debts to be paid, except for the expenses of the army that his brother Edmund, Duke of York, had led into Portugal in 1381 to back his claim to the crown of Leon and Castile. Edmund's expedition had been unsuccessful, since the King of Portugal had made a separate peace, and he had to return home; there was obviously some disagreement between the brothers over the cost of this expedition.

At the time of his death in 1399 John was married to Catherine Swynford, who had been his mistress for many years during the life of his second wife Constance. He made innumerable bequests to her, including his 'large bed of black velvet' embroidered with a circle of fetter-locks (the arms of Lancaster) and all the beds made for his body in England called 'trussing beds' (portable beds for travelling). He also leaves her 'two nouches' (pot-stands) of gold, given him by the King, plus 'all the buckles, rings, diamonds, rubies and other things, that will be found in a little box of cypress wood, of which I carry the key myself'. It is not clear from this whether the jewellery was his wife's to wear, as he kept it locked up himself, or whether the jewellery was for his own adornment. In those days, anyway, a married woman could own nothing herself.

John also left 100 marks to Newgate and Ludgate prisons in London, to be divided equally between them. This was a charitable act, and it may have been used to pay the debts of some of the prisoners or simply to improve their conditions.

In those days prisoners had to pay for their own keep in jail, or rely on charity.

John of Gaunt had eight children by his three wives and remembers them all in his will. His son by his first wife Blanch succeeded him as Duke of Lancaster and later usurped the throne as Henry IV.

One of the most famous men of the early sixteenth century was Thomas, second Duke of Norfolk, the victor of Flodden Field in 1513, where the Scottish army under James IV was annihilated. He had been created Earl of Surrey in Richard III's reign, and was attainted in 1485 when Henry VII came to the throne. After three years' imprisonment in the Tower he was received back into the king's favour and his earldom was restored; later he was made Lord Treasurer of England. He was created Duke of Norfolk, a title which had been held by his father, in 1514 and died in the same year. In his will, unusually for a subject, he often speaks of himself in the plural:

> My body to be buried in the Priory of Thetford... I bequeath CCC*l*. each for the marrying of our daughters; to oure sonne and heire apparent that shall be living at our decease, our great hangede bedd, palyd with cloth of golde, whyte damask and black velvet, and browdered with these two letters T A, and our hanging of the story of Hercules, made for our great chamber at Framlingham ... to our wife Agnes all manner of plate, jewels ... with all our goods ... to hir own behove and use. And in our most humble wise we beseech my Lord Cardinal of York good grace, of his charitie to be good and gracious Lorde unto our said wife, in hir right, that she may enjoy such things as we have given her by this our last will and testament, and we beseech his grace, that for a poor remembrance he will take our gift a pair of our gilt pots called our Skotish pots.

The Cardinal of York was Wolsey. Norfolk evidently perceived his fast rising fortunes.

Many high-born folk were greatly concerned about their

funerals. Who but a great lady like Elizabeth de Burgh, Lady Clare, a grand-daughter of Edward I, would have asked for 200lb of wax to burn round her corpse! She left innumerable legacies to her servants and, probably because she was the daughter of Joan of Acre, born to Edward I while he was crusading in the Holy Land in 1272, left 100 marks to supply five armed men if there was a crusade to the Holy Land within seven years of her death.

Lady Clare died in 1360 and was buried in Ware Church, Herts, and nine years later Lady Joan de Cobham in Kent is specifying, 'VII thousand masses to be said for my soule by the Canons of Tunbrugge (Tonbridge) and Tanfugge, and the four orders of friars in London for which they shall have xxix*l* iii*s* iv*d*'. Seven thousand masses! How was it done? Presumably twenty monks saying mass together would count as twenty masses. Joane Lady Hungerford in 1412 was more modest, asking for 3,000 masses only to be said for *her* soul.

Humphrey de Bohun, Earl of Hereford and Essex, and Lord of Brecknock, who died in 1361 at his castle of Plessey in Essex, among numerous bequests left his sister, the Countess of Devon, 'a basin in which we were accustomed to wash our heads, and which belonged to Madame, my Mother'. It is rather touching that he should remember his childhood days in his will.

Humphrey also left many jewels, for these were the days before banks, and jewels were a common form of wealth. He also wills that a chaplain 'of good condition' be sent to Jerusalem, principally for his mother and father, to say masses on the way for their souls; and that good and loyal men be sent to Canterbury to offer 40s silver for all souls and to Pomfretto (Pontefract) to offer the same amount at the tomb of Thomas, late Earl of Lancaster. The latter, a nephew of Edward I, had been beheaded for rebelling against Edward II, but proposed to the pope for canonisation by that King's son,

Edward III, who built a chapel to his memory at Pontefract.

Henry, Duke of Lancaster, surnamed Grismond from his castle in Monmouthshire, who died in 1361, wanted the King and Queen (Edward III and Philippa) to attend his funeral, and as he was a grandson of Henry III and, therefore, the King's cousin, perhaps his request was not unjustified. He was a gallant soldier, who fought at the Battle of Sluys in 1340, and Edward had once left him hostage in Flanders as security for his own debts. He died of the plague and was buried at Leicester.

Elizabeth, Countess of Northampton, in her will dated 31 May 1356, wishes to be buried in the Church of the Friars Preachers in London, and leaves 100 marks sterling to that church and 'also the cross made of the very wood of our Saviour's Cross, which I was wont to carry about me, and wherein is contained one of the thorns of his crown'.

Testators regularly stipulate for 'honest priests' and lay down conditions for their memorial services. It seems that the clergy in the Middle Ages were not always as attentive to their duties as they might have been.

William Heron, Lord Say, shows in his will the remorse that often arises at this point in one's affairs, though his sins seem quite minor, considering the age he lived in. He died in 1404 and his will reads:

> Whereas I have been a soldier, and have taken wages of the King and the Realm, as well by land as by water, and perad-venture received more than was my desert, I will that my executors pay six score marks unto the most needful men unto whom King Richard was debtor. Also having been a soldier with the Earl of Arundel, and peradventure received more than I was worthy of, I beg that 10 *l* be paid to the executors of the said Earl to be given to the poorest man to whom the said Earl was indebted.

This must have been a difficult will to carry out. William Heron died during the reign of Henry IV, and he may have

D

seen that after the death of Richard II his soldiers' arrears were not paid, and were never likely to be, by his usurper. The Earl of Arundel was, however, no friend of Richard's and had been executed in 1497.

In the early 1400s, the Lollards, followers of John Wyclif, were persecuted mercilessly, and one who recanted, Sir Lewis Clifford, KG, has left a will showing how he regretted his heresy:

> I, Lewis Clifford, false and traitor to my Lord God, and to all the blessed company of Heaven, and unworthy to be called a Christian man, make and ordaine my testament and my last will . . . I, most unworthy and God's traitor . . . recommend . . . my wretched carrion to be buried in the furthest corner of the churchyard in which parish my wretched soul departeth from my body. And I pray and charge my executors . . . that on my stinking carrion be neither laid cloth of gold nor of silk, but a black cloth, and a taper at my head, and another at my feet; no stone nor other thing whereby any man may know where my stinking carrion lieth.

Relics were frequently passed on in wills, and it seems certain that they were accepted as genuine. Some of course were, but pieces of the true cross and thorns from Christ's crown were so numerous that many wooden crosses and innumerable crowns of thorn could have been made from them. Lord Bardolph, who died in 1384 bequeaths 'to my heir male, whomsoever he be, a part of the very cross of our Lord, set in gold'.

Though married women owned nothing, widows did. Let us examine the will of a great lady, Margaret, Countess of Devon, who died in December 1391. She was the widow of Hugh Courtenay, Earl of Devon, and a grand-daughter of Edward I by his daughter Elizabeth, Countess of Hereford.

> My body to be buried in the Cathedral Church of Exeter, near the body of my lord and husband, and I desire that there be no other hearse than plain bars to keep off the press of people, and only two tapers of five pound each, one at my head, the other at my feet, without any torches or other lights;

I will that on my burial day xx *l* be distributed to poor people, to every one a groat [4d]; I will that cc *l* be distributed amongst the daughters of Knights and gentlemen, towards their marriage portions, and to poor scholars at school; to Margaret, the daughter of my son Philip, one hundred marks, to increase her portion; to William, my son, Archbishop of Canterbury, a gilt chalice and a missal; to my daughter Cobham [Margaret, wife of John, Lord Cobham] XL *l*; to my daughter Lutterell [Elizabeth, wife of Sir Andrew Lutterell] X*l*; to my daughter Engaine [wife of Sir Thomas Engaine] XL *l* with two primers and a book called Arthur de Bretagne; to my son the Earl of Devon, all my swans at Topsham; to my son Philip all the furniture of my Chapel, books, vestments, candlesticks, &c.; to my daughter Lady Ann Courtenay, a ring with a diamond; to my son Peter [Sir Peter Courtenay] my bed of red and green paly, etc.

The countess is a great deal more modest than Lady Clare (p48) in asking for only 'two tapers of five pounds each' to light her funeral, though it must have been a very dark occasion in Exeter Cathedral, in midwinter. The plain bars to keep off the press of people were a wise precaution, because if £20 was to be distributed to poor people at 4d each, then around 1,200 were likely to attend, probably more.

The old lady was generous, as the rich could be in medieval times. Charity was essential when there was no other way of looking after the poor. The dissolution of the monasteries by Henry VIII destroyed the method of charity that depended on the wealthy leaving substantial legacies to religious institutions, which dispensed it to the poor. The Elizabethan poor law illustrated that the old methods of charity had disappeared and henceforth the problems of poverty and unemployment would be dealt with officially under the parish. The bequest of £200 to be distributed among dowerless girls and poor scholars was also extremely generous and sensible. In fact the Countess was behaving like a small welfare state of her own.

Her son William became Archbishop of Canterbury on the murder of Simon Sudbury, the incumbent during the Peasants' Revolt of 1381. He was a great persecutor of the Lollards. Philip must also have been connected with the church to receive the furniture of her chapel, etc.

Topsham with its swans was in Devon. It is interesting that one daughter should have been singled out to receive the two primers and the book *Arthur de Bretagne*. They must have been in manuscript, because Caxton did not start printing until almost ninety years later. Perhaps 'my daughter Engaine' was the literary member of the family who would most appreciate the gift.

Edward, Duke of York, son of Edmund of Langley and cousin to Henry IV, was one of the most engaging rogues of the early fifteenth century. He was at the siege of Harfleur in August 1415 with the army of Henry V and made his will on 22 August. When he calls himself *'de touz pecheurs le plus meschant & coupable'* (the worst of sinners and the most blameworthy), he was not exaggerating.

He had been instrumental in murdering his uncle, the Duke of Gloucester, who died in prison in Calais; he deserted his cousin and king, Richard II; he conspired against another cousin, Henry IV, and betrayed his associates when the plot was discovered. However, he did found a college at Fotheringay and left it his crucifixes, images, tabernacles, basins, ewers, etc—except for those he had to pledge to find enough money to join Henry V in his invasion of France.

He leaves the king his best sword and dagger (*le meillour epee & le meillour dager qu j'ay*), and his wife Philippa his 'bed of feathers and leopards' with the furniture appertaining to the same and also his green bed. He wills that in the prayers and masses said for his soul the names of Richard II, Henry IV, his father Edmund, Duke of York, and his mother Isabel be joined.

The above provisions were probably due to no more than the conventional provisions of wills of the time, but there is another clause which shows that Edward could feel gratitude. He leaves £20 to Thomas Pleistede, who was kind and helpful to him when he was imprisoned in Pevensey Castle in 1405 for trying to rescue the Earl of March from imprisonment at Windsor.

Edward, despite his bad name, died a hero's death at Agincourt on 25 October 1415. He was a very fat man and, having obtained the command of the van, was suffocated in the crowd and by the heat inside his armour. He appears briefly in Shakespeare's *Henry V*:

> Enter YORK
>
> *York* My lord, most humbly on my knee I beg
> The leading of the vaward.
> *K. Henry* Take it, brave York. Now, soldiers,
> march away: And how thou pleasest,
> God, dispose the day!

He was buried in the choir at Fotheringay Church in Yorkshire. This York, whatever his successors thought, had no objection to fighting and dying for a Lancastrian King.

The mid-fifteenth century was the period of the Wars of the Roses, which were brought temporarily to an end in 1461 when the Yorkist Edward IV replaced the Lancastrian Henry VI. Edward's chief prop was the Earl of Warwick, the Kingmaker, and disagreement over policies, or, in fact, over who should rule England, eventually led Warwick to revolt, in concert with the King's brother and Warwick's son-in-law, George, Duke of Clarence. In 1469 William Herbert, Earl of Pembroke, was defeated at the Battle of Dane's Moor, near Edgecote in Northamptonshire, by Warwick and Clarence and taken prisoner. His will takes the form of a letter to his wife, dated 12 July 1469, and reads in part: 'And wyfe, that ye remember your promise to me, to take the ordre of wydowhood, as you may be the better mayster of your owne, to performe my wylle, and to help my children, as I live and trust you ... Wyfe pray for me, and take the said ordre that ye promised me as ye had in my lyfe, my hert and love'. The earl was beheaded at Northampton shortly afterwards. His wife did not remarry.

Over forty years later, in 1513, another man of action, Lord Edward Howard, also came to a violent end. He was the second son of Thomas, second Duke of Norfolk, and like all younger sons had to make his way in the world. He was distinguished both as soldier and sailor, fighting for the Archduke Maximilian in 1492 against the French, and receiving his knighthood in 1497 while on a foray into Scotland with his father. In 1509 he was appointed the king's standard bearer, and in 1512 was made an Admiral and 'Captain Commander in Chief of all the King's Ships, Captains and others to be employed in the service of the Pope for the defence of the Christian religion'. Next year he was made Admiral of England, Wales, Ireland, Normandy, Gascoigne and Aquitaine. He died in attacking some French ships in Whitsand Bay (Les Blancs Sablons) near Brest, when he and a small party of his men were separated from the rest while boarding a ship and forced into the sea by the pikes of the enemy. Before he died he threw his insignia of office, a whistle, into the sea. Just before his death on 25 April 1513, he had been made a knight of the Garter. His will reads:

... whereas that I have two bastards, I give the king's grace the choice of them, beseeching his grace to be good Lord to them, and him that the king's grace chuseth I bequeath him my bark called 'Genett' with all apparel and artillery, and L *l* to begin his stock with; and the other I bequeath to my special trusty friend Charles Brandon, praying him to be a good master to him, and for because he hath no ship, I bequeath to him c marks to set him forward in the world.

Lord Edward appoints his wife Alice and Charles Brandon

his executors, and for 'the labour of the said Charles I bequeath him my rope of bowed nobles that I hang my great whistle by, containing CCC angels; also for the strengthening of this my last will, I beseech the king's noble grace to be my supervisor, and I bequeath his grace my great whistle'. Lord Edward, like King Prasutagus, is following the familiar practice of enlisting the good offices of the powerful to ensure the execution of one's wishes after death. It does not seem, however, that the king could have received Lord Edward's whistle, because he had thrown it overboard just before his death, and if it had also been attached to the rope of bowed nobles, then Charles Brandon did not receive his bequest either.

Charles Brandon was Duke of Suffolk, and brother-in-law of King Henry after his marriage to the king's sister Mary, widow of the French king Louis XII. He also attempted to influence King Henry in his will; for although he was one of his favourites, the king was capricious and might leave the will unproved for years.

> I Charles, Duke of Suffolk, being of whole and perfite memory, considering the greate ambiguities, doubtes and questions that dayly do rise and growe in last willes . . . make this my last testament . . . I will and freelie gyve to the Kinges highnes a cuppe of golde of the value of one hunderth poundes, and the same cupp to be made of my collar of the Garter, being the value aforesaid.

He also leaves a gold cup valued at 100 marks to Prince Edward. He died on 24 August 1545, and was buried in the Royal Chapel of St George, Windsor, the chapel of the Order of the Garter.

Another example of the necessity of bribes, in this case for the Archbishop of Canterbury as well as the king, is shown in the will of Sir William Compton, Kt, one of Henry's courtiers, who tilted with his master and was Chancellor of Ireland for a time. He died in 1528 of the sweating sickness.

... to My Lord the King, from whom I acknowledge I have received all my preferment, a little chest of ivory, whereof one lock is gilt, with a chess board under the same, and a pair of tables upon it, and all such jewels and treasure as are inclosed therein, now remaining in the keeping of my wife, most humbly desiring his highness to accept thereof, as to remembrance of me; also I bequeath to my Lord the King certain specialties to the sum of M marks, being money lent to Sir Thomas Boleyn, Knt, to the intent that his highness would be so gracious to my body and children as to permit my said will to be performed as is expressed.

Sir Thomas Boleyn was the father of Ann Boleyn, Henry's future wife, and Sir William Compton is making a virtue out of necessity and paying the king out of his credits, probably feeling sure that Sir Thomas Boleyn will pay the king much more quickly than he would have Sir William himself.

However, even with these provisions, the probate, according to one of the executors, Sir Henry Guildford, was not given until the Archbishop of Canterbury, William Warham, had received 1,000 marks himself from the estate, even though Sir William had presented him with a cup and £20—not nearly enough as it turned out. This is a good example of the rapacity of the clergy. Yet, paradoxically, William Warham was said to have died, in 1532, leaving just enough to pay for his funeral expenses and debts.

Nicholas, Lord Vaux of Harrowden, who died in 1523, was a rich man, if one just considers his clothes. He was present at the wedding of Prince Arthur and Katharine of Aragon in 1501, wearing, according to Stow, 'a gown of purple velvet adorned with pieces of gold so thick and massy, that beside the silk and furs it was valued at a thousand pounds, as also a collar of SS [a Lancastrian order] weighing eight hundred pounds in nobles'. His will says, 'to my sons Thomas and William all my wearing gere, except cloth of gold and cloth of silver and tissue'.

If Lord Vaux had many more gowns like that he wore at the wedding, most of his wealth must have been in his clothes. He was a distinguished supporter of the Tudors, and had been knighted by Henry VII for his services at the Battle of Stoke in 1487. He was appointed Lieutenant of the Castle of Guisnes, near Calais (still held by the English at that time), in the first year of Henry VIII's reign and held other important posts until advanced to the peerage in 1523, but died in July of that year.

Bridget, Lady Marney, whose will is dated 1549, shows an innocent pride in her two husbands:

> My body to be buried at the end of the high altar, in the Chancel of the Parish Church of Little Horkksey [Little Horkesley, Essex], where I will that a vault of brick be made, so large that one body may conveniently be laid therein; and I will that over it be set a tomb, more than half the length of the tomb wherein Dame Katherine Finderne lieth buried, and upon the same that there be put three pictures of brass, one of myself, without any coat-armour, and upon my right side the picture of my Lord Marney, my last husband, in his coat-armour; and upon my left side the picture of my husband Finderne, in his coat-armour; and at the head or feet a scripture of brass to show the time of my decease, what stock I was of, and to what men of worship I was married.

The Duchess of Northumberland, widow of the Protector Northumberland (who failed to sustain Lady Jane Grey on the throne in 1553), left a provision to protect her modesty in her will: 'In nowise let me be opened after I am dead; I have not used to be very bold before women, much more would I be loth to come into the hands of any living man, be he physician or surgeon'. She was the mother of Robert Dudley, Earl of Leicester, favourite of Queen Elizabeth I.

Stephen Gardiner, Bishop of Winchester, an opponent of the new Protestantism and Chancellor under Queen Mary, had been a great enemy of Elizabeth I while she was still a princess,

and, had he not died in 1557, he would almost certainly have
gone to the block on her accession in 1558.

He left a 'cup of golde with a saphier in the toppe' to Queen
Mary, and 'a ring with a dyamounte not so big as he is worthie
to have' to the papal legate. Even allowing for sixteenth-
century inflation, he willed an enormous amount to be spent
on his burial: £200 on liveries for those who would see him to
the grave; £500 on his interment, presumably in appurtenances and preparing for his tomb; £300 on the tomb itself;
and £400 for the erection of 'a chauntry, that I may be provided for'.

Queen Elizabeth's principal secretary, Sir Francis Walsingham, whose position combined the posts of foreign minister,
head of the secret service and half a dozen others, probably
kept more secrets in his head than any other man in the kingdom. He was instrumental in the execution of Mary Queen of
Scots. A master of the sixteenth-century arts of intrigue and
spying, Walsingham was a worthy contemporary of Catherine
de Medici, queen mother of France. Yet he did not make a
fortune; in fact his position brought him into debt. His motive
was probably the desire for power, not wealth. 'I will that my
bodie, in hope of a joyful resurrection, be buryed without any
such extraordynary ceremonyes as usuallye apperteyne to a
man servynge in my place, in respect of the greatness of my
debtes and the meane state I shall leave my wife and heire
in . . .'

As he had lived amid secrecy and deception so did Walsingham die, his will being found by his secretaries in a secret
cabinet, presumably on the day following his death in 1590.

There is an interesting will of 1591, which, despite the
date, belongs more to the reign of James I than Elizabeth. The
testator was Richard Burnard of Knaresborough, who leaves
his cousin Dynnys Baynebrigge and his wife 'two silver goblets, worth in value XLs a piece, with my arms and name on

them, and they to have the use of them during their lives; and after their deceases I give the same goblets unto Anne and Elizabeth Faux'. To Guy Faux, brother of Anne and Elizabeth, he leaves 'two angels to make him a ring'. This Guy Faux was Guy Fawkes, whose mother was Mrs Baynebrigge, widow of Edward Fawkes, and who was discovered in 1605 preparing to blow up the Houses of Parliament.

William Cecil, Lord Burghley, Elizabeth's Lord Treasurer, died in 1597, having held high office since the beginning of her reign in 1558. He left his affairs in perfect order. His fortune amounted to £11,000 in cash, plus three houses, and a little land—not a great amount after thirty-nine years at the head of affairs.

Soldiers often make their wills before going into battle, and indeed there is a will form in the army private's paybook. Drake made one before his last expedition, as did George Villiers, Duke of Buckingham, before sailing for the Isle of Rhé in 1627. This expedition, to help the French Huguenots, was a complete failure, and Buckingham, a favourite of James I and a continuing favourite of Charles I, barely escaped impeachment on his return. He was assassinated, however, on 23 August 1628 by an army lieutenant called John Felton, who stabbed him to death. The story is told in Dumas' *The Three Musketeers*, though whether the author's explanation of Felton's reasons for the assassination is correct is doubtful.

Favourites of the early Stuarts gained great wealth, and Buckingham had a great deal to leave: £5,000 to his sister the Countess of Denbigh, but 'to be paid by my executors in such convenient time as the same may be raysed, my debtors being first payed'; £7,000 to the Earl of Northampton 'to be payed unto him by my executors forth of those sommes of money which are oweing to me by his Majesty'; £1,000 to his servant Richard Oliver; £500 each to his servants Thomas Fotherley, Edward Nicholas, and Robert Mason; and £300 to

Thomas Stockdale; but all 'to be payed . . . in such convenient tyme as the same may be raysed'. The supply of money was short in those days and it seems the duke wished the sums he willed to be collected out of his revenues and then paid, rather than they should be made up by the sale of land or houses.

He had also 'the lease of the customs of Ireland' to leave, for it was his monopoly; and he bequeathed it to his son, if living, or else to his daughter Mary. When he died the duke had one son, who became his heir, although another was born posthumously.

Buckingham's contemporary in France was Cardinal Richelieu, though he did not die until 1642. His life was as luxurious and extravagant as Buckingham's. He once had to travel from Tarascon to Paris, but could not bear the thought of the fatigue involved in travelling by litter, carriage, or horse-back—especially as it was August and very hot. So he decided to travel in a room, and had one built of wood, camouflaging its rough interior with crimson satin damask. The room was then furnished with a bed, two chairs, and a table for his secretary, and the cardinal was carried to Paris by eighteen of his guards, who were relieved at frequent intervals. As might be expected the room was rather large; many town gates on the way had to be removed, or walls knocked down, by his vanguard, so that the travelling room could pass and the mighty cardinal suffer no delay.

Apart from a bequest of 1,500,000 livres to King Louis XIII, Richelieu left all his gold and silver to one *niessce*, and much else to other nephews and nieces, though he excepts the Duchesse d'Enghien, as she had displeased him in her marriage. One nephew is left his library with the proviso that a cleaner shall be employed to sweep out the library every day and wipe the books frequently, at a yearly salary of 400 livres. The will ends with innumerable bequests to retainers.

Philip, fourth Earl of Pembroke, who died in 1650, left an amusing will:

I, Philip, IV Earl of Pembroke and Montgomery, being, as I am assured, of unsound health, but of sound memory—as I well remember me that five years ago I did give my vote for the despatching of old Canterbury, neither have I forgotten that I did see my King upon the scaffold—yet as it is said that Death doth even now pursue me, and, moreover, as it is yet further said that it is my practice to yield under coercion, I do make my last will and testament.

Imprimis: As for my soul, I do confess I have often heard men speak of my soul, but what may be these same souls, or what their destination, God knoweth; for myself, I know not. Men have likewise talked to me of another world, which I have never visited, nor do I even know an inch of the ground that leadeth thereto. When the King was reigning, I did make my son wear a surplice, being desirous that he should become a Bishop, and for myself I did follow the religion of my master; then came the Scotch, who made me a Presbyterian, but since the time of Cromwell, I have become an Independent. These are, methinks, the three principal religions of the Kingdom—if any one of the three can save a soul, to that I claim to belong: if, therefore, my executors can find my soul, I desire they will return it to Him who gave it to me.

... put not my body beneath the church-porch for I am, after all, a man of birth, and I would not that I should be interred there, where Colonel Pride was born.

Item: I give my two best saddle-horses to the Earl of Denbigh whose legs, methinks, must soon begin to fail him. As regardeth my other horses, I bequeath them to Lord Fairfax, that when Cromwell and his council take away his commission he may still have some *horse* to command.

Item: I give nothing to my Lord Saye, and I do make him this legacy willingly, because I know that he will faithfully distribute it unto the poor.

Item: Seeing that I did menace a certain Henry Mildmay, but did not thrash him, I do leave the sum of fifty pounds sterling to the lacquey that shall pay unto him my debt.

Item: I bequeath to Thomas May, whose nose I did break at

a mascarade, five shillings. My intention had been to give him more; but all who shall have seen his 'History of the Parliament' will consider that even this sum is too large.

Item: I give to the Lieutenant-General Cromwell one of my words, the which he must want, seeing that he hath never kept any of his own.

Item: I give up the ghost.

'Old Canterbury' was William Laud, Archbishop of Canterbury, who was executed in 1645 and drew up his own will while imprisoned in the Tower of London. Thomas May was known for his *History of the Long Parliament*, and died in the same year as the Earl of Pembroke. The earl seems to have brought in the church porch chiefly to express his detestation of Colonel Pride, whose birth was obscure, though he did rise to be the perpetrator of 'Pride's Purge' of the House of Commons in 1648. Two early testators, however, asked to be buried by the door: one was Richard the Fearless, the third Duke of Normandy, in the tenth century, and the other St Swithin, who died in 862. They were alike in their humility. St Swithin ordered his monks to inter his body in a 'mean place outside the door, where the foot of the passer-by might tread, and the rain water my grave'. Even then he was concerned with rain.

One of Charles II's favourites was his cousin Prince Rupert, son of his father's sister, Elizabeth, Queen of Bohemia. Poor Rupert was in the unlucky position of being a good general faced, in Oliver Cromwell, with a better. He often found himself returning to the battlefield after routing the troops opposed to him to find the day had been lost. He died in 1682 leaving property both in England and Germany. The latter went to his natural son Dudley Bart, whose mother was the Hon Anne Bart. Young Dudley only survived his father four years, being killed at the siege of Buda in Hungary in July 1686, aged twenty. The rest of his property Rupert left to his mistress Margaret Hewes, a singer and actress, and their daughter Ruperta. He confided them to the guardianship of the Earl of

Craven, who was supposed to have been privately married to his mother, the Queen of Bohemia.

One of the oddest wills was composed by Edward Wortley Montagu, who died in 1776. He was the son of Lady Mary Wortley Montagu, and his will closely resembles Lord Pembroke's:

> To my noble and worthy relation, the Earl of — I do not give his lordship any further part of my property because the best part of that he has contrived to take already. Item, to Sir Francis — I give one word of mine, because he has never had the good fortune to keep his own. Item, to Lord M— I give nothing, because I know he'll bestow it on the poor. Item, to — the author, for putting me in his travels, I give five shillings for his wit, undeterred by the charge of extravagance, since friends who have read his book consider five shillings too much. Item, to Sir Robert W— I leave my political opinions, never doubting he can well turn them into cash, who has always found such an excellent market in which to change his own. Item, my cast-off habit of swearing oaths I give to Sir Leopold D—, in consideration that no oaths have ever been able to bind him yet.

The eccentric Montagu advertised for a widow or single lady to bear him an heir, and he was on his way to meet her when he died in Padua, choking, it is said, on a chicken bone.

FIVE

ECCENTRICITY

Wills encourage eccentricity; their provisions are made known too late for us to need to be responsible. We have the last laugh. Sometimes we cannot be sure whether a will is eccentric or whether there was a shortage of paper: one man wrote his will on a door and it had to be carried into court for probate, another used wrapping paper, and the third the lid of a box.

Some testators display a whimsical humour, like the member of the Worshipful Company of Salters who died in 1605. He asked that the beadles and servants of that order should gather at St Magnus Church, London Bridge, in the first week of October every year, then proceed to the graveyard and knock on his gravestone with sticks, each one three times, and all say, 'How do you do, Brother Salter? I hope you are well'.

Eccentricity sometimes extended to the burial, especially if the surviving partner in a marriage was mean. Fisher Dilke, whose wife was sister to Sir Peter Wentworth, one of the judges of Charles I, gave her one of the cheapest funerals ever in 1660. The coffin was made of wooden palings and he beat the sexton down from a shilling to a groat (4d) for digging the grave. The bearers were friends and neighbours for whom Dilke provided a bottle of burgundy and sixpennyworth of spiced cakes. Dilke took the funeral service himself, reading a chapter of *Job* over the grave, repeating the familiar phrases

64

of the burial service, and then covering up the coffin with earth himself, using a shovel he had brought along. The whole funeral cost him 10d and a bottle of Burgundy, which must make it the cheapest funeral of all time.

Eccentricity, or anxiety, can also extend to the excessive making of wills and a plethora of codicils. The will of Dr Thomas Cheyney, Dean of Winchester, was proved in 1761, but he had been making wills on and off since 1724. He had a great fear of death, and whenever he travelled any distance he was sure to revise his will beforehand, in case he did not return.

A farmer in Hertfordshire expressed his eccentricity in refusing to be buried. In his will he stated that, as he was about to take a 'thirty years' nap', his coffin should be suspended from a beam in his barn, and the lid should not be nailed in place; the coffin should be locked but a hole left in it, so that a key could be pushed through and he could release himself when he woke up. This was in 1720 and in 1750 his nephew and heir, seeing no signs of movement, gave him another year aloft, and then buried him.

Further unusual instructions were given in the will of John Underwood of Lexington, USA, who died in 1733. The basis of his funeral was not the Book of Common Prayer but the odes of Horace. The funeral was to be held at 5pm, without the tolling of bells; no relatives were to be invited, the bier was to be painted green, and the corpse to wear his everyday clothes. Under his head was to be placed a copy of Horace and at his feet a copy of Milton. A small Greek bible was to be placed on his right hand, with his name in gold on the binding, and a smaller copy of Horace bearing the inscription 'Musis Amicus, J.U.' on his left. Under the shoulders was to be placed Bentley's edition of Horace.

These arrangements were made and after the funeral the friends who had attended were given a good supper by the

E

dead man's sister; they then recited the thirty-first ode from the first book of Horace, drank to the dead man, and retired to bed at 8pm. Underwood had left his fortune to his sister, on condition she carried out his instructions, and the friends £10 each, requesting them not to wear mourning. Once the grave had been filled in and turfed over, the friends gathered round it and concluded the ceremonies by singing the last verse of the twentieth ode of the second book of Horace.

More amusing than eccentric was the will of Daniel Martinett of Calcutta:

In the name of God, I, Daniel Martinett, of the town of Calcutta ... make this my last will and testament... To avoid Latin phrases, as it is a tongue I am not well versed in, I shall speak in plain English.
First. In the most submissive manner I recommend my soul to Almighty God.
Secondly. Now as to worldly concerns, In the following manner:—As to this fulsome carcase having already seen enough of worldly pomp, I desire nothing relative to it to be done, only its being stowed away in my old green chest, to avoid expense; for as I lived profusely, I die frugally.
Thirdly. The undertaker's fees come to nothing, as I won them from him at a game of billiards in the presence of Mr. Thomas Morice and William Perkes, at the said William Perkes' house, in February last. I furthermore request ... that the Rev. Mr. Henry Butler read the prayers which are customary and also preach a funeral sermon ... but as my finances are low, and cannot conveniently discharge his fees, I hope he will please accept the will for the deed.
Fourthly. To Henry Vansittart, Esq., as an opulent man, I leave the discharge of all such sums of money (the whole not exceeding 300 rupees) that I shall stand indebted to indigent persons in the town of Calcutta.

Fifthly to *eighthly*, Martinett bequeaths his sincerity, modesty, 'all the thoughts I shall die possessed of', and his worldly assurance to four legatees, then winds up:

As I have lived the make-game of a modern gentleman, being a butt for envy and a mark for malice, by acting a little out of the common road, though, thank God, never in a base way, I hope I may die in sincere love and charity to all men, forgiving all my persecutors, as I hope for forgiveness from my Creator.

As it lies not in my power to bequeath anything to my relations at home, I shall say nothing concerning them, as they have not for these six years past concerned themselves about me; excepting that I heartily wish them all well, and that my brother and sisters may make a more prosperous voyage through this life than I have done.

Henry Vansittart was Governor of Bengal at that time (1760-64) and it is said that he good-naturedly paid Martinett's debts.

Dennis Tolam of Cork, who died in 1769, left his sister-in-law four old stockings, his nephew Michael Tarles two stockings and a green nightcap, Lt John Stein a blue stocking and a red cloak, cousin Barbara Dolan an old boot with a red flannel pocket, and Hannah his housekeeper his cracked water jug. The legatees were disgusted with the will, and Hannah kicked her water jug across the floor in a temper—but it broke and coins rolled out. Thereupon, the others looked at their bequests more closely and found money hidden away in them all.

Sometimes it is a good idea to make your will and let everyone know what is in it for them, as a wealthy bachelor found in 1790 when he was taken ill. He informed all his servants that he had left them reasonable legacies, but that they would be doubled, as would the doctors' fees, and paid immediately on his recovery. Never was a man waited on and examined with better care. He soon recovered and paid up as he had promised. There is no record, however, of how many times he repeated this practice.

Samuel Gillam in 1793 showed a great suspicion of undertakers, and cast around until he found an 'honest man':

... whereas I think it a very great absurdity and the most egregious folly to make the deaths and burials of persons to be an occasion of pomp and show, I do hereby order and desire my funeral may be performed in such manner as may be barely decent, but no more, and that the expense thereof do not exceed including the parochial fee £20, and that William Brent do undertake the same. I give unto the said William Brent as a legacy £10. I verily believe he is an honest man.

Many people, having a contempt for death or funerals, or being public-spirited, have left their bodies to science. Jean de Labadie willed in 1674: 'It may be that my body, in which I have suffered great physical pain ... may be usefully opened and examined, and that some lessons may be drawn from it advantageous to the prolongation of other lives'; and in 1759 the Bishop of Winchester stated: 'It is my express desire that my body be opened so far as to see whether any appearance in it may be of use to my fellow creatures ...'

The Anatomy Act of 1832 stated that the executor might allow the body to go for anatomical examination unless the deceased had opposed the idea, or the family or relatives objected. Today, one is positively useful in willing kidneys or hearts to science.

The next will is eccentric in its vagueness, and in its hatred of the English. It was written by a Frenchman in 1779:

> Item, I leave to M. l'Abbé Trente-mille hommes twelve hundred livres a year; I do not know him under any other name, but he is an excellent citizen, who assured me at the Luxembourg that the English—that fearsome nation, which dethrones its sovereigns—will soon be detroyed.

In defence of the English, one must say that the French had dethroned and beheaded their own sovereign before the end of the century. But how were the executors to find the Abbé 'Trente-mille hommes' or 'Thirty-thousand men'? The testator had taken a walk every day in the Allée des Larmes in the Luxembourg, and perhaps he had met the Abbé there. Sure enough he had, though he had never learnt his name and only knew him from his assertion, often made, that 'Thirty-thousand men would suffice to beat the English'. The nickname was enough to identify the patriotic Abbé, and secure him his legacy.

John Redman of Upminster, Essex, who died in 1798, was, on the contrary, a revolutionary. His will reads:

> To Mr French of Harpur Street . . . a set of Tom Paine's 'Rights of Man', bound with common sense, with the answers intended by the longheads of the law, fatheads of the church, and wiseheads of an indolent usurping aristocracy. . . To that valuable friend of his country in the worst of times, Charles Fox, Member for Westminster, five hundred guineas. To each of the daughters of Horne Tooke, five hundred pounds.

Since 1789 the whole western world had been inflamed by the ideas of the French Revolution, and Paine, Fox and Tooke were supporters of those ideas. Fox, indeed, was the great Parliamentary opponent of William Pitt the Younger. Tom Paine had supported the American Revolution and Horne Tooke, a leader of the revolutionary Corresponding Society, had been tried for treason, but acquitted, in 1794.

Wills, however, are not often concerned with international affairs, and in 1810, when the struggle with Napoleon was at its height, Mr Tuke of Wath, near Rotherham, Yorkshire, was more concerned with arrangements for his funeral: he left 1d to every child attending his funeral (about 700 came), 1s to every poor woman in Wath, 10s 6d to the bellringers to ring a peal of grand bobs while he was being buried, and sufficient money to allow for four dozen penny loaves to be thrown down from the church roof on every Christmas Day for ever. He did not forget his relations and dependants: an old woman who had tucked him up in bed every night for eleven years received an annuity of a guinea per annum, and his natural daughter received an annuity four times as large. His old and faithful servant, Joseph Pitt, received an annuity of £21 per annum, and the church received two brass chandeliers and £20 for a set of new chimes. A far cry from Napoleon and the battlefields of Europe.

His will was only mildly eccentric, perhaps, like the will of Mrs Maria Redding of Branksome, Hants, in 1870:

> If I should die away from Branksome, I desire that my remains after being duly placed in the usual coffins [ie first a leaden and then an elm one], be enclosed in a plain deal box, and conveyed by goods train to Poole. Let no mention be made of the contents, as the conveyance will then not be charged more for than an ordinary package. From Poole station let it be brought in a cart to Branksome tower, and it will be found the easiest way to get the coffin out of the house will be to take out one of the dining-room windows.

A very practical will, indeed!

A New Yorker, who died in 1880, found an equally practical yet wildly eccentric way to spite his heirs:

> I own seventy-one pairs of trousers, and I strictly enjoin my executors to hold a public sale at which these shall be sold to the highest bidder, and the proceeds distributed to the poor of the city.
>
> I desire that these garments shall in no way be examined or meddled with, but be disposed of as they are found at the time of my death ...

One might have thought the heirs would have smelt a rat and bought up the pairs of trousers themselves, for after the sale each pair was found to contain $1,000 sewn into the lining. But the heirs had no suspicions and the trousers were sold, the money thereby going to strangers. One might call it a rough and ready form of charity, for presumably secondhand trousers would be bought only by poor men.

The next will illustrates the lawyer's nightmare (or delight perhaps) of preparing a will that can be read in more than one way. Mrs Hook, the wife of a major who had served with the

East India Company, had received a legacy which was to continue as long as she was 'above ground'. The loophole is obvious. After her death Major Hook kept her coffin in a glass case well above ground for the next thirty years, enjoying the legacy until he died himself at the age of seventy-five. Such an event must have made the patron saint of lawyers turn in his grave. Lawyers do have one. He is St Yves, who was a lawyer himself; he was born in Brittany in 1253 and canonised by Clement VI, a fourteenth-century pope, at Avignon.

Perhaps American wills can be even more eccentric than British. An example is the will of John Reed, gas-lighter at the Walnut Street Theatre, Philadelphia, for forty-four years during the nineteenth century. Being only a gas-lighter, and seeing hundreds of plays performed during his working life, he evidently wished to appear on the stage himself; but unlike the clown wanting to play Hamlet, he wanted the minor part of Yorick, the clown:

> My head to be separated from my body immediately after my death: the latter to be buried . . . the former, duly macerated and prepared, to be brought to the theatre, where I have served all my life, and to be employed to *represent* the skull of Yorick —and to this end I bequeath my head to the properties.

John Reed wished his remains, at least his skull, to perform a useful purpose after his death, and other testators have recoiled from the idea of their bodies crumbling into dust, preferring cremation. Disposal of the dead has always been one of the key differences between cultures. In the western world today there is a swing from burial to cremation; but in the nineteenth century the latter practice was generally frowned on. William Kinsett, however, a Londoner who died in October 1855, attempted it:

> . . . believing in the impolicy of interring the dead amidst the living, and as an example to others, I give my body, four days after death, to the directors of the Imperial Gas Company,

London, to be placed in one of their retorts and consumed to ashes, and that they be paid ten pounds by my executors for the trouble this act will impose on them for so doing.

If this was impossible, then Kinsett wanted to be buried in the family grave at St John's Wood Cemetery 'to assist in poisoning the living in that neighbourhood'. In those days it was almost impossible to be cremated, undertakers not catering for a practice so at odds with the conventions of the time. The difficulty had been overcome in the previous century, in 1769, by a Mrs Pratt of George Street, Hanover Square, London, who was burned to ashes in her grave in a new cemetery that had been built near the Tyburn turnpike.

Mr S. Sanborn, a hatter, wanted his body to be of some use after his death, and when he died in 1871 he bequeathed it to Harvard University for the special use of the two professors of anatomy, one of whom was Oliver Wendell Holmes, desiring 'his remains should be preserved in the Museum of Anatomy at Harvard, after having been dealt with in the most scientific and skilful manner known to the anatomical profession'. So far so good, but from then on the will becomes highly eccentric. He requests that his skin should be converted into two drumheads, 'to become the property of his distinguished friend and patriotic fellow-citizen, Warren Simpson, drummer of Cohapel', on condition that he should, on 17 June every year at dawn, 'beat on the said drum the tune of Yankee Doodle on Bunker's Hill'. Sanborn also wanted Pope's 'Universal Prayer' and the Declaration of Independence to be inscribed on the drumheads. Once these instructions had been carried out,

> The remainder of my body useless for anatomical purposes to be composited for a fertiliser to contribute to the growth of an American elm, to be planted in some rural thoroughfare, that the weary wayfarer may rest, and innocent children may play beneath its umbrageous branches rendered luxuriant by my remains.

One famous man, of course, who wished his remains preserved after his death was Jeremy Bentham (1748-1832) and his wishes were carried out by his friend Dr Southwood Smith. Bentham wished his body to be present at occasions when his friends met, and, once his dead face was covered with a wax mask, this was done. Eventually his body was moved to University College, London, where it remains in skeleton form to this day.

To insert a note of comedy, one of the most amusing wills was the work of a Dutchman called Klaës of Rotterdam, who died about 1875. He was called the King of Smokers and it is estimated that during his life he smoked over 4 tons of tobacco and drank over 500,000 quarts of beer. In his will he invited all the smokers of Holland to his funeral, where each was to be presented with 10lb of tobacco and two new pipes engraved with his name, his arms and date of death. He asked that his mourners should keep their pipes going throughout the funeral service and that they should then empty the ashes on his coffin. The local poor people who obliged were to have 10lb of tobacco and a cask of beer annually. He ordered his coffin to be lined with the cedar wood from his old cigar boxes, a box of French caporal and another of Dutch tobacco to be placed at the foot of his coffin, and his favourite pipe laid by his side, with matches, flint and steel, and tinder, as he said that once he had departed this world there was no knowing what ways of lighting one's pipe were available in the next. No doubt he still puffs away in some smoker's heaven.

The last thing any of us would be likely to do nowadays would be to leave our money to the government, considering that in our lifetime that body must collect at least half our earnings in taxes. But in 1875 taxes were not so high, and Thomas Alexander Mitchell, who had been MP for Bridport in Dorset, left £240,000 (after seeing that his wife was well provided for) to the Metropolitan Board of Works in London.

It is perhaps unfair to call this will eccentric, for Mr Mitchell's intentions were charitable, and he left the legacy, 'to the Chairman for the time being of Her Majesty's Board of Works to be applied by the said Board for any such charitable purposes benefiting the City of London in which I have passed my life, as the Board for the time being shall in their absolute discretion think best'.

Finally, let us take an eccentric Scot, which is almost a contradiction in terms. He left two young daughters, and bequeathed each of the girls her weight in £1 notes: the elder collected £51,200 and the younger £57,344. The mathematically minded reader could work out the weight of each girl. It is interesting to speculate why he adopted this method: perhaps he loved the fatter younger daughter the more, yet did not want to offend the elder by saying so; or perhaps they had plagued him about the distribution of his wealth, and he adopted this method in exasperation. More likely it was a joke.

WILLS IN VERSE

> All lawyers like to take a rest
> Like most of us, and still.
> The average lawyer's happiest
> When working with a will.

Lawyers have never had a good press. We feel we get our money's worth from other professional men, but lawyers, no: they have invented the law just to lift money from our pockets. Perry Mason used to say that a lawyer accused of a crime who conducts his own case has a fool for a client. Lawyers believe the same rule applies to the testator, as is made clear in the following poem:

THE JOLLY TESTATOR WHO MAKES HIS OWN WILL

Ye lawyers who live upon litigants' fees,
And who need a good many to live at your ease;

Eccentricity

Grave or gay, wise or witty, whate'er your degree,
Plain stuff or State's Counsel, take counsel of me:—
When a festive occasion your spirit unbends,
You should never forget the profession's best friends;
So we'll send round the wine, and a light bumper fill
To the jolly testator who makes his own will.

He premises his wish and his purpose to save
All dispute among friends when he's laid in his grave;
Then he straightway proceeds more disputes to create
Than a long summer's day would give time to relate.
He writes and erases, he blunders and blots,
He produces such puzzles and Gordian knots,
That a lawyer intending to frame the thing ill,
Couldn't match the testator who makes his own will.

Testators are good, but a feeling more tender
Springs up when I think of the feminine gender!
The testatrix for me, who, like Telemaque's mother,
Unweaves at one time what she wove at another.
She bequeaths, she repeats, she recalls a donation,
And ends by revoking her own revocation;
Still scribbling or scratching some new codicil,
Oh! success to the woman who makes her own will.

You had better pay toll when you take to the road,
Than attempt by a by-way to reach your abode;
You had better employ a conveyancer's hand,
Than encounter the risk that your will shouldn't stand.
From the broad beaten track when the traveller strays,
He may land in a bog, or be lost in a maze;
And the law, when defied, will avenge itself still,
On the man and the woman who make their own will.

This is probably true, if you have a lot to leave, though it does not apply to the simple wills of the majority. Probably, from its reference to a toll on a road, this poem was written in the late eighteenth or early nineteenth centuries.

Wills in verse are legal as long as they express themselves unequivocally. One of the early rhyming wills was William

Hickington's, which was proved in the Deanery Court at York
in 1770. It is short and sweet:

> I, William Hickington,
> Poet of Pocklington,
> Do give and bequeath,
> As free as I breathe,
> To thee, Mary Jarum,
> The Queen of my Harum,
> My cash and my cattle,
> With every chattel,
> To have and to hold
> Come heat or come cold,
> *Sans* hindrance or strife,
> Though thou art not my wife.
> As witness my hand,
> Just here as I stand,
> The twelfth of July,
> In the year Seventy.

Another eighteenth-century will was Monica Swiney's, in
rather a different metre:

> Of this I never will repent,
> 'Tis my last will and testament,
> If much or little—nay, my all—
> I give my brother, Matthew Gall;
> And this will hinder any pother
> By sister Stritch or Mic, our brother;
> Yet stop! should Mat die before Mic,
> And that may happen, for Death's quick,
> I then bequeath my worldly store
> To brother Mic for evermore;
> But should I outlive my brothers,
> It's fit that then I think of others.
> Matthew has sons, and daughters too,
> 'Tis all their own, were it Peru.
> Pray, Mr. Forrest, don't sit still,
> But witness this as my last will.

Mrs Swiney's will is so light-hearted that one knows she was

on good terms with her relations. William Ruffell of Shrimp-
ling, Suffolk, however, takes the opportunity to tilt at lawyers
and castigate his brother-in-law in his will, written in 1803:

> As this life soon must end, and my frame will decay,
> And my soul to some far-distant clime wing its way,
> Ere that time arrives, now I free am from cares,
> I thus wish to settle my worldly affairs,
> A course right and proper men of sense will agree,
> I am now strong and hearty, my age forty-three;
> I make this my last will, as I think 'tis quite time,
> It conveys all I wish, though 'tis written in rhyme.
> To employ an attorney I ne'er was inclined,
> They are pests to society, sharks of mankind.
> To avoid that base tribe my own will I now draw,
> May I ever escape coming under their paw.

Ruffell leaves his land and property to his nephew, Ezra
Dalton, and continues:

> To my loving, kind sister I give and bequeath,
> For her tender regard, when this world I shall leave,
> If she choose to accept it, my rump-bone may take,
> And tip it with silver, a whistle to make.
> My brother-in-law is a strange-tempered dog;
> He's as fierce as a tiger, in manners a hog;
> A petty tyrant at home, his frowns how they dread;
> Two ideas at once never entered his head.
> So proud and so covetous, moreover so mean,
> I dislike to look at him, the fellow's so lean.
> He's ne'er behaved well, and, though very unwilling,
> Yet I feel I must cut him off with a shilling.
> My executors, too, should be men of good fame;
> I appoint Edmund Ruffell, of Cockfield, by name;
> In his old easy chair, with short pipe and snuff,
> What matter his whims he is honest enough;
> With Samuel Seely, of Alpheton Lion,
> I like his strong beer and his word can rely on.

Finally, there is the nice will of Sarah Smith, which must be

early twentieth century, as she talks about her old-age pension.
One feels that the exigencies of rhyming led Mabel to receive
the 'parlour chair and table'.

> I, Sarah Smith, a spinster lone,
> With little here to call my own,
> Few friends to weep at my decease,
> Or pray my soul may rest in peace,
> Do make my last and only will,
> (Unless I add a codicil),
> My brother Sam to see it done
> For he's the right and proper one.
> I give the kettle that I use
> At tea-time, and the little cruse
> That holds hot posset for a guest
> To Martha, for she's homeliest;
> Perhaps she'd like the picture too
> In needlework of Auntie Loo
> (So like her), and of Uncle Jim,
> She always was so fond of him.
> Then there's the parlour chair and table,
> I give them both to you, dear Mabel,
> With love, and when you sit thereat
> Remember there your Sarah sat.
> My poor spectacles will be
> More use to you, alas, than me,
> So take them, Polly, and they may
> Perhaps sometimes at close of day
> Grow dim when memories arise
> Of how they suited Sally's eyes.
> Pussy will not be with you long,
> But while she lives do her no wrong,
> A mug of milk beside the fire
> Will be the most that she'll desire.
> There's little else I have to mention,
> For, when I've spent my old-age pension,
> Not many crowns disturb my sleep,
> But what there is is Sam's to keep:
> He's been a brother kind and good

Eccentricity

In all my days of solitude.
And so farewell: no word of ill
Shall stain my last and only will;
But, friends, be just and gentle with
The memory of Sarah Smith.

SIX

GREAT MEN

The great men of history tend to lead the most conventional of private lives. They are not the framers of the great eccentric wills. The interest in their bequests lies in the light they can shed on their personal lives, the small details of their household, their feelings for their family, their financial situation.

Nobody could doubt the greatness of Plato and Aristotle. Plato, an Athenian, died in 348 BC, aged about eighty, leaving two farms to his son Adimantes, plus three minas (300 drachmas) in cash, a silver vase, a silver cup, a gold pendant and a gold ring. Adimantes also received three minas that his father had lent to Euclid the gem-engraver, probably as an investment, with four slaves and all his chattels. Plato freed his slave Diana in his will, and died without debts.

Aristotle seems to have been better off, but he had been tutor to Alexander the Great. He had earlier been Plato's pupil and died in 322 BC at Calchis, leaving three executors in charge of his affairs until Nicanor came of age. Aristotle laid down that his daughter was to marry Nicanor when she was old enough, and Nicanor was also to take charge of his son Nicomachus. If Nicanor died too soon, Theophrastus was to carry out his duties.

Aristotle recommends Herpylis to his executors, and if she

marries (and his executors are to make sure she does not disgrace Aristotle by marrying below his station), she is to receive one talent of silver (100 minas), three slaves in addition to the one she already has, and the youth Pyrrhaeus. She may live in Calchis if she wishes, and there she may have the suite of rooms adjoining the garden; and if she opts for Stagyra (in the north-west Aegean) she may occupy his ancestral home. Whichever she chooses, the executors must furnish it suitably.

He frees his slave Ambracia, and to make sure that her freedom is not just a descent into poverty, leaves her 500 drachmas (or 5 minas) and a slave for herself. He makes various other bequests, including slaves, and orders that the children of his slaves shall serve his heirs and be freed when they grow up if they deserve it. Greece was now ruled by Macedonian kings, but even in the great days of Greek democracy a century earlier, slaves had formed a considerable part of the population. After conquering a city or island, or defeating the enemy in battle, the prisoners were frequently slaughtered; selling them into slavery can only be considered a forward step from that policy.

Aristotle concludes by mentioning some statues he has ordered, some of which were animals to be dedicated to Minerva and Jupiter; and asks that the bones of his wife Pythias be placed in his tomb, as she had requested.

From Greek philosophers to a Roman Emperor, the first and probably the greatest, Augustus, who died in 14 AD, having previously deposited his will in the Temple of the Vestal Virgins, probably the safest place in Rome. He was, anyway, their chief as Pontifex Maximus.

One of the problems of the civil power is to prevent a military takeover. This was especially true of the Roman period when so many of the later Roman emperors were brought to power by the support of their forces.

But Augustus, though his own position was secure, and his

heir Tiberius succeeded without disturbance, was prudent enough to leave each soldier of his 9,000 strong bodyguard *millia nummorum* (1,000 sesterces), each soldier of the urban cohorts (3,000 men) in Rome half that amount, and each legionary *trecentos nummos* (300 sesterces). As there were twenty-five legions at the time, each one consisting of about 5,000 men, the total amount came to about 48 million sesterces. Even so the soldiers grumbled at the smallness of the legacies and some even mutinied.

That great sailor Sir Francis Drake, the victor over the Armada, lived for seven years after its defeat, and died on a fruitless expedition to the West Indies with his old sailing companion, Sir John Hawkins. Drake made his will just before leaving on his expedition 'wherein I am about to hazard my life as well in the defence of Christes Gospell as for the good of my prince and countrie . . .' It was a vain effort of two old men trying to recapture the glory that was theirs only a few short years before. Hawkins died, and then Drake on 28 January 1596. The Elizabethan age was coming to an end, only the Queen, among its stalwarts, living into the seventeenth century.

England's greatest admiral, Nelson, in his will, written on the day of his death at the Battle of Trafalgar, 21 October 1805, tried to remind his countrymen of the services of his mistress, Lady Hamilton, to England:

> In sight of the combined fleets of France and Spain, distance about ten miles. Whereas the eminent services of Emma Hamilton, widow of the Right Honourable Sir William Hamilton, have been of the very greatest service to my king and country, without ever receiving any reward from either our king or country. *First*, that she obtained the King of Spain's letter, in 1796, to his brother the King of Naples, acquainting him of his intention to declare war against England: from which letter the Ministry sent out orders to the then Sir John

Jervis to strike a stroke, if the opportunity offered, against either the arsenals of Spain or her fleets. That neither of these was done is not the fault of Lady Hamilton: the opportunity might have offered.

Secondly. The British fleet under my command could never have returned the second time in Egypt, had not Lady Hamilton's influence with the Queen of Naples caused a letter to be written to the Governor of Syracuse, that he was to encourage the fleet being supplied with everything, should they put into any port in Sicily. We put into Syracuse, and received every supply; went to Egypt and destroyed the French fleet. Could I have rewarded these services, I would not now call upon my country; but as that has not been in my power, I leave Emma, Lady Hamilton, therefore, a legacy to my king and country; that they will give her an ample provision to maintain her rank in life.

These are the only favours I ask of my king and country, at this moment when I am going to fight their battle ...

Put not your faith in princes, nor in prime ministers or lords of the Admiralty either. Nelson had a premonition he was going to die, and Lady Hamilton's services, not to mention his own, might surely have been worth a discreet pension for her. But no. Nelson was given a magnificent funeral, and his will was disregarded. Emma Hamilton went abroad to die in France in 1813. Her daughter by Nelson, Horatia, lived until 1881. The influence of the greatest of men, and Nelson was probably the greatest naval commander the world has ever known, dies with them.

Nelson died at the moment of victory. Perhaps his great antagonist Napoleon would have preferred to die at the moment of defeat at Waterloo in 1815, but, instead, he lived another six years in exile on the island of St Helena in the South Atlantic and died on 5 May 1821. In his will he says, 'I die prematurely, assassinated by the English oligarchy', and asks for his ashes to be buried on the bank of the Seine. They were, in fact, taken back to France in 1840, during the reign of Louis Philippe, and buried under the dome of the Invalides in Paris. It is estimated that Napoleon caused the deaths of 500,000 French soldiers in his campaigns, but this has never lowered him in French esteem. He blames his defeats on others: 'The two unfortunate results of the invasions of France when she had still so many resources, are to be attributed to the treason of Marmont, Augerau, Tallyrand and La Fayette'. Marmont and Augerau were two of his marshals, Tallyrand was a political wizard who survived Napoleon to serve the French monarchy again, and La Fayette was the hero of the American War of Independence and the early days of the French Revolution.

Acting like an emperor to the last, Napoleon left bequests amounting to 6 million francs, though there was no money to pay them. He gave 10,000 to the French officer Cantillon, who had been tried for attempting to assassinate the Duke of Wellington but acquitted. Napoleon's view was that Cantillon 'had as much right to assassinate that oligarchist, as the latter had to send me to perish upon the rock of St Helena'.

The 'oligarchist', the first Duke of Wellington, was a very cool character indeed, unlikely to have been moved by anything Napoleon had to say. He had been born in 1769, three months before Napoleon, and, though strictly Anglo-Irish, was and remains England's most successful general; probably Marlborough was the better tactician but his success did not equal Wellington's. The Iron Duke wrote his will in Paris in longhand in 1818, and it begins in bloodcurdling fashion :

An attempt having been made to assassinate me on the night of the 10th instant which may be repeated with success, and being desirous of settling my worldly affairs and there being no professional person at Paris to whom I can entrust the task of drawing my will, I now draw it in my own hand writing, hereby revoking all former wills, particularly one likewise in my own hand writing made in the year 1807 previous to the Expedition to Copenhagen.

The duke makes provision for his wife and sons, and in case his sons are not alive to inherit and have left no heirs, lists his nephews in order of precedence and their heirs. One of his possessions was Apsley House, which still stands, as a museum, at Hyde Park Corner in London.

He was forty-nine at that time, and left a list of his assets at the end of his will; having started with very little, he had amassed a considerable fortune:

Schedule of what I possess annexed to my will of the 17th Feby 1818 according to the best of my recollection.

	L. s. d.
Duchess of Wellington's fortune in the hands of Lord Longford and Colonel Pakenham	6,000
Due to me by Mr Pole	3,000
Due to me by Mr Smith	2,700
Due to me by Sir H. Wellesley I believe	2,000
In Exchequer Bills in Mr Coutts hands I believe	130,000
In the Funds 70,000£ I believe at 80	56,000
	———
	199,700

W.

The duke lived until 1851, when he was eighty-two, and died without making any further will; Lord Raglan and a John Parkinson of Lincolns Inn Fields were called in to swear that it was indeed in the duke's handwriting. Administration of the will was granted in 1853 to Arthur Richard, second Duke of Wellington, the duke's son.

That other great British war-leader, Sir Winston Churchill, died in 1965, leaving £304,044. He asked to be buried in the 'Churchyard of Bladon, near Woodstock in the County of Oxford', and that the gold cigar case presented to him by the first Earl of Birkenhead (F. E. Smith) should be given to the present earl at his death. His house, Chartwell, had already been presented to the National Trust before he died.

He is mentioned in David Lloyd George's will, dated 1944, in a codicil that says: 'I bequeath free of duty to my said wife the picture of Marakeesh painted by The Right Honourable Winston Spencer Churchill . . .' Lloyd George left £140,000 when he died in 1945.

T. E. Lawrence, famous as Lawrence of Arabia, died on 19 May 1935 in the military hospital at Bovingdon Camp, Wool, Dorset, after a motor-cycle accident. In his will he leaves his two executors £100 each and 'a copy of Shelley's Poems (Kelmscott Edition in three Volumes as published by William Morris)'.

Benjamin Franklin, who died in 1790, had been American ambassador in Paris and instrumental in bringing France in on the American side during the War of Independence. His will, however, shows a certain amount of embarrassment at a gift he had received from Louis XVI, though it also shows his admiration for the first president of the United States:

> The King of France's picture, set with four hundred and eight diamonds, I give to my daughter, Sarah Bache, requesting, however, that she would not form any of those diamonds into ornaments, either for herself or daughters, and thereby countenance the expensive, vain and useless pastime of wearing jewels in this country.
>
> My fine crabtree walking-stick, with gold head curiously wrought in the form of a cap of liberty, I give to my friend, and the friend of mankind, General Washington. If it were a sceptre, he has merited it and would become it.

Franklin was also a philanthropist, leaving £2,000 to be lent at interest to 'married apprentices of upright behaviour'.

George Washington himself, a Virginian, died on 14 December 1799; his will contains a section dealing with his slaves:

> Item. Upon the decease of my wife, it is my will and desire that all the Slaves which I hold in my own right shall receive their freedom. To emancipate them during her life, would, though earnestly wished by me, be attended with such insuferable (sic) difficulties on account of their intermixture by mar-

riage with the dower Negroes, as to excite the most painful
sensations, if not disagreeable consequences from the latter
while both descriptions are in the occupancy of the same proprietor; it not being in my power, under the tenure by which
the dower Negroes are held, to manumit them. And whereas,
among those who will receive freedom according to this device,
there may be some who from old age or bodily infirmities, and
others who, on account of their infancy, that will be unable to
support themselves, it is my will and desire that all who come
under the first and second description, shall be comfortably
clothed and fed by my heirs while they live; and that such of
the latter description as have no parents living, or, if living,
are unable or unwilling to provide for them, shall be bound by
the court until they shall arrive at the age of twenty-five years;
... The Negroes thus bound are (by their masters and mistresses) to be taught to read and write and to be bro't up to
some useful occupation, agreeable to the laws of the commonwealth of Virginia, providing for the support of orphan and
other poor children—And I do hereby expressly forbid the sale
or transportation out of the said commonwealth of any Slave
I may die possessed of under any pretence whatsoever.

Washington in his will freed his mulatto servant, William
Lee, but as the man was crippled directed that he might
remain in his present situation if he so wished. He left him
an annuity of $30 in remembrance of 'my sense of his
attachment to me, and for his faithful services during the
Revolutionary War'.

Washington clearly would have liked to free all his slaves
but was prevented by the fact that some were part of his wife's
dower, and the constitution of the State of Virginia stood in
the way. By the beginning of the nineteenth century many
civilised American slave-owners were embarrassed and
ashamed at the thought of owning other men and women, but
law and custom prevented them from behaving in a humane
manner and freeing them. Also the United States of America
was such a novel conception that the State (Virginia in the

case of Washington and most of the early American presidents) received much more of their loyalty and affection.

Franklin's 'fine crabtree walking-stick' remained in the family, for George Washington left it to his brother Charles.

The third president of the United States and another Virginian, Thomas Jefferson, who died in 1826, was also concerned with slavery in his will:

> I give to my good, affectionate, and faithful servant Burwell, his freedom, and the sum of three hundred dollars, to buy necessaries to commence his trade of glazier, or to use otherwise, as he pleases.
>
> I give also to my good servants John Hemings and Joe Fosset, their freedom at the end of one year after my death; and to each of them respectively, all the tools of their respective shops or callings; and it is my will that a comfortable loghouse be built for each of the three servants so emancipated on some part of my lands convenient to them with respect to the residence of their wives... I also give to John Hemings the service of his two apprentices Madison and Eston Hemings, until their respective ages of twenty-one years, at which period, respectively, I give them their freedom; and I humbly and earnestly request of the legislature of Virginia a confirmation of the bequest of freedom to these servants...

It appears that the wives of the three freed slaves were not freed with them, and that the president of the United States had to sue humbly to the State of Virginia to get these provisions accepted.

Slavery is mentioned as late as 1852 in the will of Henry Clay, American politician and statesman, who died on 29 June. Its first clause is a reminder of the relics of the Middle Ages:

> I give to my friend Henry T. Duncan my ring containing a piece of the Coffin of General Washington.
>
> In the sale of any of my slaves I direct that the members of families shall not be separated without their consent.
>
> My will is and I accordingly direct that the issue of all my female slaves, which may be born after the 1st day of January

1850 shall be free at the respective ages of the males at twenty eight and of the females at twenty and that the three years next preceding their arrival at the age of freedom, they shall be entitled to their hire or wages for those years or the fair value of their services to defray the expense of transporting them to one of the African Colonies and furnishing them with an outfit on their arrival there. And I further direct that they be taught to read, to write and to Cipher, and that they be sent to Africa.

Clay's provisions for freeing his slaves were overtaken by events, for all slaves became free at the end of the American Civil War in 1865. It is interesting that as late as 1852 the solution to the slaves' future to many thinking men was to send them to Africa, or simply to return them to the homeland of their ancestors. This situation was of course impossible in 1865, for the South was broken by the war, and the North was prepared only to free the four million slaves, not to do anything more about them.

The idea of repatriation had started under the presidency of James Monroe (1816-24), when the state of Liberia was founded. The capital is indeed called Monrovia. The first freed American slaves landed there in 1822, but when the country became independent in 1841, only 3,000 slaves had settled there. And it is ironic that they themselves carried on a slave trade until it was suppressed by the British in 1850.

America's president during the years of the Civil War, Abraham Lincoln, who was assassinated by the actor John Wilkes Booth in 1865, died intestate, leaving $110,295. His salary as president was $25,000 per annum, and Congress, with the punctiliousness of accountants, paid his salary up to the day of his death only. His fortune was divided equally between his wife and two sons.

Another great American president, Franklin D. Roosevelt, who died on 12 April 1945, just before the surrender of Germany in World War II, left an estate of $1,852,308. Death duties, just called tax in the USA, amounted to $45,993.

Great men are fairly common, though many of their wills are not particularly interesting; but great women are as rare as snowdrops in July—Joan of Arc, Queen Elizabeth I, and Florence Nightingale. All three of these ladies can be said to have had 'greatness thrust upon them'—the first by 'voices from Heaven', the second by her position as Queen at a stormy period of English history, and the third by her insistence that at least one part of the Crimean War should be conducted with efficiency and humanity. Florence Nightingale (1820-1910) was, of course, the great pioneer of nursing, and as befitted her profession left one particular provision in her will: 'I give my body for dissection or postmortem examination for the purposes of Medical Science . . .' She was, however, buried in East Wellow, Hampshire, among her ancestors, having refused the honour of burial in Westminster Abbey.

SEVEN

CHARITY

Charitable organisations mostly collect their funds through flag days, bequests, covenants or endowments. Testators are generous; take a look at the column in *The Times* headed 'Latest Wills', which appears almost every day, and you will see. It is difficult to estimate how much is left to charity every year in Great Britain, but it might be as much as £100 million.

Britain's most famous philanthropist of recent years was Lord Nuffield, head of Morris Motors, who died in 1963. In his will he left just over £3,250,000, but long before that, in 1943 and 1944, he had allocated £10,000,000 to set up the Nuffield Foundation; this amount was represented in 1970 by 39,565,848 five-shilling shares in the British Leyland Motor Corporation Ltd. The objects of the Foundation, which operates in Great Britain and the Commonwealth, are (1) the advancement of health and the prevention of sickness by medical research and teaching, (2) the advancement of social wellbeing, (3) the care and comfort of the aged poor, and (4) the advancement of education; and since its inception the Foundation has distributed nearly £29,000,000.

Probably the most famous European philanthropist was Alfred Bernard Nobel (1833-96), of Nobel Prize fame. He was a Swede and the inventor of the explosives dynamite and nitroglycerin. He left a prize fund of $8,400,000 whose interest was to be divided annually and distributed to the following five persons: those making the most important discovery or perfecting the most important invention in (1) physics, (2) chemistry and (3) physiology or medicine; in literature the writer (4) producing the most distinguished work of an idealistic tendency; and (5) the person who has most or best promoted the interests of universal peace. The first four categories are awarded by the academies of Sweden, and the fifth by the Norwegian Storthing or Parliament. Nominations for the prizes come from foreign academies and universities, Scandinavian professors, former recipients of prizes and distinguished men. Some famous winners have been the Curies, Bernard Shaw and T. S. Eliot, and the prizes have ranged from £11,000 to £22,000, according to the funds available.

Disputes over charitable bequests rarely come into court, but an exception occurred in 1970 in St Helier, Jersey, concerning the will of a former MP, Sir John Wardlaw-Milne, who died in 1967. Sir John had left a large amount of money to be divided among ten charities, one of which was called the London Boys' Home, but no charity of that name could be found. It was stated in court that the Gordon Boys' School in Surrey, which had been formerly called the Gordon Boys' Home, was the charity in question, and that when the will had been typed out the word 'London' had been inadvertently substituted for 'Gordon'.

On the other hand, the counsel for the St Christopher's Fellowship, whose policy was to supply homes for working boys in London, maintained that this charity was more likely to be the one intended, since it was based in London and Sir John had been deeply concerned with the welfare of children there.

This was a puzzler for the court, which eventually decided that there had been a typing error and that the Gordon Boys' Home was the charity intended.

In the Middle Ages a man of property often left a good proportion of his income to pious uses, and this meant the religious houses, which did much to help the poor. In 1278 Edward Grobbe ordered that his ship *Blewbottle* be sold for the maintenance of a charity in the chapel of St Mary de Berkinggechurch, London. And in the same year Stephen Le Gras ordered all his rents in five parishes to be sold, along with all his other goods, houses and rents, named or not named, and the money received from the sales to be distributed by his executors to the poor. Part of Stephen's will was put aside on a legal nicety at the instance of his sister Margery, for he had listed his property in particular and then in general, which was superfluous, so administration was granted only upon the property particularly mentioned.

At this time wills in London were proved and recorded at the Court of Husting, a word going back to the Danes, and meaning just 'a court in a house'. The court still functioned as late as 1688, but by then most of the richer citizens had moved out of the City of London, and there was no penalty for not enrolling one's will. In 1302 it was made obligatory for the testator to use his seal on his will. Wills could be refused probate if the witnesses prevaricated (they could be pilloried for that), or if the executors did not present it promptly, or if there were suspicious erasures or interlineations. Noncupative wills were particularly susceptible to fraud.

London Bridge was frequently in need of repair, and public-spirited citizens would leave sums of money for this purpose in their wills: Giles le Cutepointer half a mark in 1303, Geoffrey Davy 6d and Anastacia Bunting half a mark in 1300, Hugh de Bedeforth 40d in 1304, Roger de Lauvare 25d in 1307.

Richard Whittington, Lord Mayor of London (Dick Whittington of the pantomime), bequeathed money for the rebuilding of Newgate Gaol when he died in 1423. The gaol was the responsibility of the City Fathers, and was tumbledown throughout much of the Middle Ages.

William Haute of Canterbury, in May 1462, left a number of relics:

> I bequeath one piece of that stone on which the Archangel Gabriel descended, when he saluted the Blessed Virgin Mary, to the image of the Blessed Virgin Mary of the Church of Bourne, the same to stand under the foot of the same image. I bequeath one piece of the bone of St. Bartholomew to the Church of Waltham; one piece of the hair cloth of St. Catherine the Virgin; and a piece of the bone of St. Nicholas to the Church of the Augustine Friars [in Canterbury].

This was charity in an indirect form, for the churches concerned would benefit from increased congregations coming to see the relics.

The richer the testator, the more charitable could he be. Walter Blount, who died in 1474, was the Yorkist Lord Treasurer to Edward IV, who gave him the title of Lord Mountjoy:

> I will ... that my executors purchase land of the yearly value of x*l* and appropriate them to the Hospital of St. Leonard, situated between Alkemonton and Bentley, to pray for the souls of my ancestors ... also I ordain that the master of that hospital for the time being shall find continually seven poor men ... also I will that the master for the time being shall pay weekly unto these seven poor men II*s*. IV*d*.; also that every one of them, at the time of his election shall be of the age of fifty and five years at the least, and that they shall have seven kine going within my park at Barton, and seven loads of wood yearly for their fuel, to be taken within my lordships of Barton, Alkmonton, and Bentley; or other lordships in Appletree Hundred, in the county of Derby; also I will that the said master shall, every third year, give unto each of those seven poor men a gown and a hood of white or russet of one suit, one time white and another time russet, the gown to be marked with a tayewe [St Anthony's cross] of red, and I ordain that none of these poor men go a begging, upon pain of re-

moval from the hospital; likewise I will that every of them be obliged to say daily our Lady's Psalter, twice, within the chapel of the said hospital.

Another charitable testator was John Sixtini, physician and friend of Erasmus and Dean Colet, and rector in his time of Egglescliffe in the diocese of Durham, and Haccomb in the diocese of Exeter. He died in 1519.

I bequeath one moiety of my estate in Frisia to the poor of Bolsward, and the other half to the monastery of Owgocloyster, near Bolsward, in which my sister is professed, but I will that my brother Albert shall have one half part of the profits of the same during his life; to the reparation of the Church of Eglescliffe, in the diocese of Durham, though I had not one penny for dilapidations from my predecessor the Bishop of Ely x *l* sterling; I will that xx *l* be distributed among the poor inhabitants of the said parish, for the purchase of tools and other instruments for their rustic labours, at the discretion of my executors; to the honour of God and St Blaze, towards the reparation of the church of Hakkomb, in the diocese of Exeter, though I had not a penny for the delapidation of the same xv *l*; to be distributed for exhibitions to poor scholars in the universities of Oxford and Cambridge xl *l* . . .

Sixtini seems to have been a Frisian or North German from his will. He came off badly over 'dilapidations' at his churches, and he cannot forbear to mention the fact, though he leaves money to them both.

George Butler of Coleshill, Warwickshire, was concerned with lodgings for poor travellers in his will of 2 September 1591. He arranged that the rents of his house in the lower part of the town, and also the rents of a house and lands in Gilson, should be used to keep an almshouse in repair and buy furniture when necessary. The house was to put up any poor travellers who desired it, but only for one night, except under exceptional circumstances. He orders care to be taken that men and women do not lodge near each other, and that one or two poor persons might be allowed to stay rent free if they were willing to clean the house and take care of those in transit.

Butler's will was quite simple, in contrast to Matthew Wall's of 1595. The latter ordered that his tenements and lands in the parish of Braughing in Hertfordshire should be levied of a yearly payment of 20s to be distributed by the minister and churchwardens on St Matthew's day (21 September), as follows:

	s	d
To the sexton, for making up the grave yearly and ringing the bell	1	10
To twenty boys aged between six and sixteen, a groat apiece (5d)	8	4
To ten aged and impotent people of the parish, 3d each	2	6
To sweep the path from his house to the church gate yearly	1	0
To the crier of Stortford to proclaim yearly that he had left his estate to a Matthew, or William, Wall, 'as long as the world should endure'		8
To the parish clerk at Hallingbury for the same		8
To the minister and churchwardens to see his will performed	5	0
	20	0

The amount can only be made to balance by assuming that the Elizabethan groat was worth 5d, though it is generally assumed to have been worth 4d.

The charitable impulse of Charles Jones of Lincoln's Inn, whose will is dated 17 January 1640, was frustrated by the Civil War, which broke out in 1642. He directed that a hospital should be erected for twelve poor men at Pullhelly (Pwllheli) and that first his father, and then his uncle and his heirs should run it. He left certain lands giving £50 per annum to finance the project. His reason for providing the hospital was that his deceased wife, father, mother, sister, brother

Griffith, himself and servants had been saved from the sea there; also, when he had been about three or four he had been miraculously led from a house 'that was instantly cast down by the moultringe of an hill near thereunto, and therein nine persons and Christians were killed by reason thereof'. The almshouse was not, in fact, built until over 100 years later, in 1760, by his descendant William Price.

Another useful bequest, which was fulfilled, was that of John Wardall, whose will was dated 29 August 1656, during the Commonwealth. He left the Grocers' Company a tenement called the White Bear in Walbrook, London, so that they would have funds every year to pay the churchwardens of St Botolph, Billingsgate, £4 to provide 'a good and sufficient iron and glass lantern' with a candle to be fixed on the north-east corner of the church for travellers to see their way to and from the waterside during the night. The candle was to be lit from the feast of St Bartholomew (24 August) to Lady Day (25 March), and the sexton of St Botolph's was to have £1 out of the £4 for looking after the lantern.

Another Londoner, John Cooke, made a similar bequest in 1662:

> For the maintenance of a lantern and candle, to be of eight in the pound at the least, to be kept and hanged out at the corner of St. Michael Lane, next Thames Street, from Michaelmas to Lady-day, between the hours of nine and ten o'clock at night, until the hours of four or five in the morning, for affording light to passengers going through Thames Street or St. Michael's Lane, £1.

Wardall left four times as much as Cooke, so the latter's candle was probably much inferior, though at 'eight in the pound' it must have weighed 2oz.

The mysterious murder in the seventeenth century of Sir Edmund Bury Godfrey has never been cleared up. He disappeared on 12 October 1678, and his body was found five

G

days later in a ditch on Primrose Hill, run through with his own sword and possibly strangled. His death was fastened on by Titus Oates and the anti-catholic hysterics, who claimed he had been foully murdered by romanish priests. Their own guilt has long been suspected. Godfrey was a charitable man, whose will was proved the following April:

> As for the Charity which I have for some years bestowed on the poor of the parish of St. Martin's in the Fields aforesaid, viz. 10/- in bread on every Lord's Day or on some day at the beginning of each week, my will is that my executors ... do jointly and severally take care and continue to do the same by themselves for the space of ten years from and after the time of my decease ... And I do further will that the Charity by me given of 2/- per week in bread to the poor of the parish of Selling [Kent], being the place of my birth ... be weekly continued to be given.

No section of the community has been worse treated over the centuries than the men of the British Navy; Queen Elizabeth I allowed her crews to starve after the victory over the Armada, Nelson's sailors were press-ganged into the fleet, and in fact it was not until quite late in the twentieth century that the men in the Royal Navy received anything like the pay and conditions they deserved. One 'seaman's friend' was Francis Millington of Wandsworth, which was in Surrey in the seventeenth century, but is now part of London. In his will of 1692 he left £500 on trust to the Governors of Christ's Hospital to buy freehold land within 100 miles of London whose rents should support poor seamen or watermen of Wandsworth aged fifty or over who had lost a limb or limbs at sea or had been wounded and disabled from getting a livelihood. They were also to be given blue cloth coats every year on Michaelmas Day, and if there was a shortage of applicants the charity could be extended to cover other poor men of similar age, or even younger.

One hazard of the sailor's life was that his ship might be

captured and himself be sold into slavery. Such a fate was possible up to the eighteenth century, so much so that in 1725 Thomas Betton of Hoxton Square, Shoreditch, which was then in Middlesex, left most of his property (about £22,000) to the Ironmongers' Company upon trust to be invested and

> One full half-part of such interest of the whole estate to be paid yearly, for ever, to the redemption of British slaves in Turkey or Barbary.
> One full fourth-part yearly for ever unto charity schools in the city and suburbs of London, where the education is according to the Church of England.

The remaining quarter was to go to the Ironmongers' Company for administrative expenses.

This bequest came in very handy, and one of the first transactions released 135 Britons from the Barbary States in 1734; on their return they dined with the King, Lords of the Admiralty, and members of the Ironmongers' Company in Ironmongers' Hall. Between 1734 and 1826 the company spent £21,088 8s 2½d in redeeming captives.

As slavery died out, however, the company found that its income from Betton's bequest was more than sufficient for its purpose, and in 1829 the Attorney-General filed an information against them saying that as they had not redeemed any slaves for many years and as there were now treaties between England and Turkey and the Barbary States prohibiting all dealing in slaves, the money might be used for some charity the testator would have approved of. The company had to make some sort of defence and argued that even now some parts of the Barbary States were not effectively controlled by their rulers and that English sailors shipwrecked on the north African coast were sometimes held captive. As late as 1825 they had paid the sum of £320 6s 9d for the release of the crew of a vessel wrecked north of Cape Canton, and for paying their passage home, the men having been, in effect, bought from their captors by the Emperor of Morocco.

The company had to admit, however, that they had more than they needed for such redemptions, for the net income now amounted to £1,700 a year. The matter was eventually settled in the Court of Chancery, and in 1841 the Lord Chancellor directed that the money could be switched to supporting schools subscribing to the Church of England faith in England and Wales, each school not receiving more than £20 a year.

One of the largest disbursements ever in the eighteenth century, or in any other century for that matter, was that of a Portuguese Jew named Pineido, who lived in Amsterdam. He distributed it as follows in his will:

1 Five 'tons' of gold to the city of Amsterdam. (A 'ton' was 100,000 florins or roughly £10,000).

2 A loan of 1½ million florins to the city without interest for ten years.

3 To every Christian church in Amsterdam and the Hague 10,000 florins, and to one particular church in the southern quarter of Amsterdam 20,000 florins.

4 To each Christian orphanage in the two towns 10,000 florins.

5 To the poor of Amsterdam forty shiploads of peat.

6 To the orphan who first leaves a particular orphanage 1,000 florins and to the next 600.

7 To the synagogue in Amsterdam 2½ 'tons' of gold.

8 To the Portuguese orphanage 3,000 crowns.

9 To the Government 10 'tons' of gold at 3 per cent on condition that the interest was paid to the Jews living in Jerusalem, though the capital should belong to the Government always.

10 To the German synagogue 5,000 florins.

11 To his nephew Ovis 31 'tons' of gold, with house and appurtenances.

12 To his widow 10 'tons' of gold.

13 To other relations 10,000 crowns each.

14 To neighbours assisting at his funeral 100 ducats each.

15 To every unmarried person of either sex at his burial 100

florins, and to every Christian priest in Amsterdam and the Hague 100 crowns, and to every sacristan 50 crowns.

It is impossible to calculate how much was distributed but it must have amounted to well over £500,000. It would be comparable to a bequest of, say, £10,000,000 today.

One late nineteenth-century will echoed medieval wills in disposing of a relic. William Sands Cox of Leamington, who died in 1876, left the Cottage Hospital at Moreton in the Marsh in Worcestershire £3,000 plus the chair in which Charles I had sat at his trial before Parliament in Westminster Hall. He had inherited it from William Sands, who had got it from a Lady Fane of Little Compton, Warwickshire, a direct descendant of Bishop Juxon. The bishop had attended Charles at his execution, and later became Archbishop of Canterbury.

One interesting donation to the fine arts was the Chantrey bequest, which came into operation in 1878 on the death of Lady Chantrey, widow of Sir Francis Chantrey, the sculptor, who died on 25 November 1841. According to his will, after his wife's death £3,000 a year was to go to the Royal Academy, plus £300 to the President and £50 to the Secretary—for buying paintings and sculptures executed in Great Britain by artists of any nation. Sir Francis hoped that the government would build a gallery to house these works, but this has never been done, though the money of the bequest has been extensively used.

Charity is international. An Englishman, James Smithson, left $500,000 to found the Smithsonian Institution in Washington DC. The foundation was to be 'an establishment for the increase and diffusion of knowledge among men', and its foundation was contingent upon a nephew of Smithson's dying without issue, legitimate or illegitimate. The establishment of the Institution was delayed for ten years by Congress, but finally the trust was accepted and a board of regents to administer it appointed. The US Weather Bureau stems from this foundation.

As Smithson, an Englishman, had benefited the Americans, so did George Peabody, an American, benefit the English. He was born in 1795 in Massachusetts and died in 1869; and in his youth he had fought against England in the war of 1812. During his life he gave away nearly $10,000,000 to charity, $3,000,000 of which was allocated to the education of the poor in the southern states of America. In London he founded Peabody & Co and spent another $3,000,000 on model tenements for the poor of London, most of which are still standing. Lack of houses for the poor in nineteenth-century London was chronic, and this shortage was aggravated by the great numbers of houses knocked down in bringing the railways into the city, and by the development of commercial thoroughfares. Peabody's tenements were occupied by the slightly better off working men, but they performed a very useful service in relieving overcrowding.

His service to the country was recognised, and when he died in London, unmarried, in 1869, Queen Victoria attended his funeral and Gladstone was one of his pallbearers. His body was taken back to America in HMS *Monarch*.

Peabody's example influenced another American, John Hopkins, a financier who died in Baltimore in 1873. He allocated $7,500,000 to found Johns Hopkins University and Hospital, having created corporations to run them before his death. The hospital was instructed to take both black and white patients, which was revolutionary at the time, just a few years after the end of the American Civil War, and in Maryland, which, though on the Union side, bordered on Virginia and had been a slave state.

AMERICAN FOUNDATIONS

There are fifteen thousand of these in the USA today; most are small, but one hundred and seventy have assets of more than $10 million and fifteen assets of over $100 million each. Probably the best known are those institutions bearing the names of Rockefeller, Carnegie and Ford.

All these benefactors followed the golden rule of philanthropy—doing it yourself. John D. Rockefeller, Sr (1839-1937), founder of Standard Oil, gave up active participation in his company's affairs in 1896 and devoted himself to charitable work, though he had, of course, given away a great deal before then. His method was to put up half the money for a project on the understanding that others would provide the rest. In this way he gave $600,000 towards the foundation of the University of Chicago in 1890, others finding $400,000; altogether he gave that university $35 million, which can only be described as princely.

Other philanthropies were the Rockefeller Institute for Medical Research in 1901 (now the Rockefeller University), and in 1902 the General Education Board for promoting education in the USA, particularly in the South, both white and negro. When the latter was dissolved in 1965, it had distributed nearly $325 million. The Rockefeller Foundation was established in 1913 'to promote the well-being of mankind throughout the world' and in the fifty-seven years of its existence to the end of 1970 it had distributed $998 million towards medical research and public health, agricultural research in the poorer parts of the world, the arts, fellowships for scholars and scientists (including numerous Nobel prize winners), education, foreign universities, and studies of environmental problems like pollution. One scientific project, towards which the foundation and two other Rockefeller philanthropies gave $6 million, was the 200in telescope on Mt Palomar in California.

An arts project was the Shakespeare Festival at Stratford, Ontario. A major medical discovery was a yellow-fever vaccine.

John D. Rockefeller, Sr, gave away the staggering sum of $531 million, about four-fifths of that to the Rockefeller Foundation, the General Education Board, the Laura Spelman Rockefeller Memorial (named after his wife), and Rockefeller University, and the rest to numerous colleges and universities and other good causes. His son, John D. Rockefeller, Jr (1874-1960), was equally generous, devoting his life primarily to charitable work. He was associated with his father in many of his foundations, and did a great deal of fund-raising during both wars, the USO (the American combination of NAAFI and ENSA) being largely his creation. He also contributed substantially to the Protestant church, though he believed in interdenominationalism, to the conservation of natural resources, and parks. In 1923 he founded the International Education Fund, to which he gave more than $21 million; and he also gave $5,250,000 to the United Negro College Fund.

One of the projects in which he was most interested was the restoration of eighteenth-century Williamsburg, the colonial capital of Virginia, to which he contributed over $56 million. An international project was his giving $8,515,000 in 1946 for the purchase of land in New York for the UN building. He also built the famous Rockefeller Centre.

In 1940 his five sons founded the Rockefeller Brothers Fund, to which John D. Rockefeller, Jr, gave £58,981,000 and half his estate in his will. Altogether John, Jr, gave away $561 million, which, added to his father's donations of $531 million, makes a grand total of $1,092 million—a staggering sum!

One man who influenced the first John D. Rockefeller's thinking on philanthropy was Andrew Carnegie (1835-1919), who emigrated from Scotland in 1848 and, by his foundation of the Carnegie Steel Company, launched the US steel industry at Pittsburgh. At the age of sixty-five he sold out his interest to J. P. Morgan for $400 million and devoted himself to giving away his fortune. His view was that personal wealth beyond that needed to supply one's family should be regarded as a trust fund 'to be administered for the benefit of the community'. This opinion was very similar to that of Pope Leo XIII (1878-1903) in an encyclical on the conditions of the working class:

> It is a most sacred law of nature that a father should provide food and all necessaries for those whom he had begotten. . . In no other way can a father effect this except by the ownership of lucrative property which he can transmit to his children by inheritance.
>
> Man should not consider his outward possessions as his own, but as common to all so as to share them without hesitation when others are in need. When what necessity demands has been supplied and one's standing fairly taken thought for, it becomes a duty, not of justice (except in extreme cases), to give to the indigent out of what remains over.

Carnegie had in fact been disposing of his fortune before he retired, his first donations being given around 1870 to his native town of Dunfermline in Scotland. Later he set up seven philanthropic and educational bodies in the USA, of which the Carnegie Corporation was one, and several in Europe. One of his favourite schemes was free libraries as a means of self-education, which he promoted from 1881, subsequently building 2,509 of them throughout the English-speaking world at a cost of more than $56 million.

The Carnegie Corporation was founded in 1911 to promote the advancement and diffusion of knowledge and understanding among the people of the USA, and a subsequent gift allows 7 per cent of its income to be devoted to the Commonwealth. Its original endowment was £135 million and its present market value about $280 million. It is mainly concerned with education and certain aspects of government affairs, and throughout its life it has distributed $381,090,869 in the USA and $30,606,812 in the Commonwealth, making a total of $411,697,681.

Mr Carnegie established numerous other foundations, including the Carnegie Foundation for the Advancement of Teaching (1905), which had by mid-1970 distributed over $81 million, largely in retirement pensions to teachers, and with the corporation, had founded the Teachers Insurance and Annuity Association, a non-profitmaking insurance company concerned with teachers' pensions, whose assets had grown astronomically to $2,900 million by 1969. Other organisation include the Carnegie Institute and the Carnegie-Mellon University at Pittsburgh, numerous Carnegie Hero Funds in Europe and the USA for recognising heroic acts in peace time, and trusts for the universities of Scotland and for Dunfermline (1903).

One of Andrew Carnegie's philanthropic schemes that did not reach fruition was his suggestion in 1912 that the Carnegie Corporation should provide pensions of $25,000 per annum for ex-Presidents of the USA or their unmarried widows. But the public disapproved and the plan was dropped. In his will, however, Mr Carnegie left annuities to Mrs Cleveland (widow of Grover Cleveland), Mrs Edith Roosevelt (widow of Theodore Roosevelt), and ex-President Taft.

Andrew Carnegie's personal bequests amounted to more than $308 million, yet in his will he still managed to leave a further $10 million to the Carnegie Corporation, and Mrs Carnegie in hers left it valuable property on Fifth Avenue, New York.

John D. Rockefeller, Sr, was oil, Andrew Carnegie was steel, and Henry Ford was, of course, motor cars. In 1936 Henry Ford and his son Edsel established the Ford Foundation, and when Edsel died in 1943, and Henry Ford in 1947, they left the major portion of their estates to it. In the beginning it supported charitable and educational work in Michigan, in which lies the Ford works at River Rouge, Detroit, but in 1950 it became a nationwide and international philanthropy. The foundation's original assets consisted of shares in the Ford Motor Company, but these have been run down from almost 90 per cent to about 20 per cent, on the principle that it is better not to have all one's eggs in one basket.

The foundation is worth $2,390 million. Since 1936, the year of its inception, its grants and expenses have totalled $3,800 million, distributed to 6,165 institutions and organisations in the USA and eighty-three foreign countries—an amount overtopping income by $1,400 million. The greatest distribution came in 1966—$354,006,530—when the President, McGeorge Bundy, did admit that the foundation would have to cut down a bit. In 1970 it distributed $235 million, which included $30 million over a five-year period to a Police Foundation, reflecting American concern over law and order, to make grants to police departments for investigating improved approaches to law enforcement.

It also supports research into problems of the environment and pollution, and is particularly strong in its support of the arts, backing music, professional and amateur, the theatre, ballet, the visual arts, and public television in the USA as an alternative to the commercial channels.

A third of the Ford Foundation's budget goes to its International Division, a particularly high proportion for an American Foundation, or any other for that matter. Much of its support goes to the countries of the Third World—on education and research in Asia and the Pacific, on supporting agriculture in backward countries, on searching for an answer to the population problem in countries like India, Pakistan and Brazil, whose populations are likely to double in the next twenty to thirty years. The Ford Foundation has a great deal of money and is not afraid to spend it.

Charity

In the USA private giving is much higher in proportion to government welfare than in Great Britain. But American government spending on welfare is increasing by leaps and bounds every year. The great foundations are experts in supporting good causes, and their independence allows them a greater flexibility and initiative than government agencies.

EIGHT

TROUBLED AND
TROUBLESOME WILLS

TROUBLED

Wills have often been written under stress or in situations of danger. Men have written their wills while trapped in sunken submarines or in blocked coalmines. For the years 1348 and 1349, when the Black Death was at its height, the Rolls of the Court of Husting in London are full of wills outdated by the rapid deaths of the legatees. Nicholas de Barton's will, dated 19 January 1349, was enrolled in the February following, and it mentions his wife Alice; but before the will was enrolled she was dead. Hugh de Stokwell, whose will was dated 8 April 1349, soon followed his father Richard to the grave, for the latter's will had been dated 4 April 1349, and both were enrolled by the court on the same day.

Another bad year for the plague was 1515. In July the will of Gefferey Salesbury of Leicestershire was witnessed by the priest only, 'and no more for fear of the plague of pest'.

In 1603 the plague killed 41,000 people in London alone, one of whom was Francis Mountstephen, whose will was proved on 29 August. It was in the form of a letter:

> I repose trust in you, brother Nicholas, concerning the executorship. Brother Nicholas, since it hath pleased God to visit

me with his rod, which I pray God that rod I may take with patience, you writ me concerning the suit which I ever well liked... For that bond of £50 you speak of I am content you should have it, upon condition that you would see the rest equally bestowed on the rest; but, if your discretion think it good, let my two younger sisters have somewhat the greater share, for they have the most need withal. Remember my uncle Baldion because of my promise. And so referring the rest to your discretion, I commit you to the Lord God... whom I desire to release me from my pains which I intolerable do bear. From the pesthouse, this two and twentieth of August, 1603. Your loving brother F.M. If it please God that I do die, I owe to Edward Smith 10/-: I pray you pay it for me. F.M. I pray you take 8/- of Elizabeth Price when she cometh to town. Witnesses, Henry Chitham, Keeper of the pesthouse, Rose Gibb and Robert Smith.

In November of the Plague year 1625, Edward Blackerly, a clothworker, could not find a scrivener to record his will until he was so weak that he was unable to complete it.

There are some affecting wills from the fearful year of 1665. John Grover wrote on 1 September:

My mother desired me on her death bed to be a brother to my sister Mary Grover, and if she lived to give her in money ten pounds, and a gold ring which was my mother's... If it should please God to take me away, and my sister alive, I desire she should have all that is her's... John Hunt will be one to see that it is not all baffled away but carefully looked to for the good of my poor sister.... And my desire is that she be defrauded of none, but that care be taken for the child's bringing up. As for my burial accordingly to the discretion of my overseers: if healthy times decently, if other times according to their appointment. This I writ myself for fear I should be deprived by sudden death.... The trunk at Mr. Hall's and chest and box are top full of the best of linen and other things, and my trunk is top full at the tavern... If I die I pray let this be engrossed and put for my will in court.

John Grover's will was accepted and proved on 13 May 1666.

A will proved a few days earlier, on 4 May 1666, was that of

Henry Mabank, which was in the form of a letter to his mother outside London:

> Dear Mother, my duty to you remembered, and my love to my brothers and sisters and to Mr. Rudd and Mistress Rudd and Billy and to Henry Chandler, hoping you are all in good health as I am at this present writing, thanks be to God. Dear Mother, my desire and will is, that if you never see me more that my brother George and sister Betty and sister Ann shall have £100 which is upon bond equally divided between them... Dear Mother if it please God that I live till the 7th of August there will be £10 due to me from my master and £3 due the 20th of August upon bond. This £13 I will leave to your disposing. I am not afraid of the sickness, yet it is very near our house. I pray excuse me from writing every week; you shall hear of my welfare in Mrs. Rudd's letters. So in haste I rest your dutiful son till death. Henry Mabank. July the 20th, 1665.

Death in action was probably better than death from plague, for with the latter the only action to be taken was to flee to the countryside. James Dixon, a seaman who had been seconded from HMS *Pearl* to a sloop hired by the Royal Navy and called the *Jane*, made a noncupative will just before the *Jane* encountered a pirate ship called the *Adventure* in November 1718. He was a bachelor, and evidently had no family ashore, declaring before several reliable witnesses:

> Messmate, being going to engage, which God knows whether of us shall live, but if it please God it is my misfortune to die first, I desire that you would take care and demand all my wages, prize money and what shall be due to me from this day, the longest liver of us to take all.

There is something appealing about this bold declaration of a brave seadog. The messmate referred to was a sailor called Evender Mackever. Shortly after James Dixon had made this will, the *Jane* engaged the pirate, and he was shot and killed.

James Dixon may have well felt that he was fighting in a

111

good cause, but poor Lt-Col Frederick Thomas, who made his will on 3 September 1783, had no such comfort:

> I am now called upon, and, by the rules of what is called honour, forced into a personal interview of the most serious kind with Colonel Cosmo Gordon: God can only know the event, and into His Hands I commit myself... I... declare this to be my last will and testament... In the first place I commit my soul to Almighty God, in hopes of His mercy and pardon for the irreligious step I now (in compliance with the unwarrantable customs of a wicked world) feel myself under the necessity of taking.

Frederick Thomas had evidently been forced into a duel, which proved fatal to him. His will was probated eight days later.

TROUBLESOME

One of the institutions likely to cause trouble was the Court of Chancery. It seemed to do its best to twist the testator's meaning into something he never intended. Horace Walpole, in a letter to Sir Horace Mann, expressed the common feeling about the court in the eighteenth century:

> Sir William Rowley is dead; he has left £6000 a-year—to whom do you think... to his great-grandson! To his son who had never disobliged him, he gives but £800 a-year, the same to his grandson; all the rest and his savings to his grandson's heir! It is positively tempting the Court of Chancery to do a thing they well might—set aside such an absurd will.
>
> Do not doubt of it; the law makes no bones of wills. I have heard of a man who began his will thus: 'This is my will, and I desire the Court of Chancery will not trouble themselves to make another for me'.... Oh, but it did though.

Wills were causing trouble way back in thirteenth-century London. In 1280 Robert Hardel left William, his son and heir, his main house, plus bequests to his wife, his son Roger, and his daughters Beatrice, Johanna, and Isabella. But William was

in no hurry to hand over the bequests, and his sister Johanna
and her husband Simon de Lardar had to bring up the matter
before the Court of Husting, accusing William of withholding
the will from probate. The court thereupon made William
produce the will and distribute the legacies.

Another interesting case, in 1299, concerned the will of
Angnes de Colevile, who left Roger de Corby, a chaplain, her
tenement in the parish of St Dionisius Bakcherche, in London.
William de Berton, a clerk, disputed the will on the grounds
that the tenement was not hers to will away as she had only a
life interest in it. He said it should be his on her death, though
we do not know what relation he was to her. He also claimed
that the testatrix had made another will when she had been of
sound memory, implying that she was senile towards the end
of her life; and that Roger de Corby had destroyed this will
and persuaded her to make another in his favour. Martin le
Tayllour also came forward with claims. Corby, however, must
have won the case, for in his own will of 1303 he leaves the
property to be sold for pious uses and for supporting Reginald,
his father.

The rolls of the Court of Husting show that it settled the
cases brought before it with a speed and efficiency lacking in
today's courts of law.

Another will in dispute was Alexander Heyrun's, dated
1308. He had left a tenement to Thomas, son of Margery, his
late wife, and to Mariota, Thomas's sister, on condition that
'they keep clean and maintain their moiety of a latrine pertain-
ing to the said tenement'. But the will was held back from
probate by one of the executors, William Peverel, who wished
to prevent the legatees having the property. However, it was
eventually brought before the court and admitted.

A will whose request might have caused some trouble, or at
least a ringing in the ears, was that of John Teryngham, who
died in February 1500:

I will that the great bell shall ring from six of the clock in the morning until six at night, on the day that I am buried . . .

It is probable that the will of Matthew Tindal (1657-1733) was forged. The testator—advocate, deist and pamphleteer—was an old man in 1733 when he left Oxford and came to live in London at the house of a Mrs Lucy Price. One of his neighbours was a writer called Eustace Budgell, who often visited him in the few months before his death in August 1733. Budgell, a relative of Joseph Addison, had had a career of great promise early in the eighteenth century, and had written for the *Spectator*; but his promise remained unfulfilled. He involved himself in numerous lawsuits, and claimed to have lost £20,000 in the South Sea Bubble; and by 1733 was a Grub Street hack, editing a bankrupt journal.

Tindal's nephew, Nicholas, expected to be his uncle's heir, but when the old man died, Mrs Price produced a will leaving over £2,000, some manuscripts and property to Budgell, and making Nicholas Tindal the residuary legatee. But there was no residue, and it appeared that £1,800 had already been lent to Budgell. Tindall produced a pamphlet accusing Budgell, but failed to upset the will, though Budgell's character, not good even then, was further blackened. Everyone thought that, having borrowed old Matthew Tindal's money and being unable to pay it back, he, with Mrs Price's help, had forged the will, or persuaded the old man to sign a forged will, to save himself from prosecution.

He protested his innocence, but four years later travelled to Dorset, took out a boat, after filling his pockets with stones, and jumped overboard. He was deeply in debt at the time, and the coroner's jury returned a verdict of suicide while insane.

A will that caused real trouble, and was meat and drink to the Court of Chancery, was that of J. M. W. Turner, probably England's most distinguished painter, who died in 1851. Its layout was confused, but his intention evidently was, after

114

leaving certain legacies, to bequeath his paintings to the nation and the residue of his estate to an institution for the support of 'poor and decayed' legitimate male artists born in England and of English parents. The amount at issue was £140,000, and the will was disputed by Turner's next of kin. Five years' wrangling followed in the Court of Chancery, until, in 1856, a judgement was arrived at: the real estate was given to the heir-in-law, the paintings to the National Gallery, £1,000 allocated for the erection of a monument to Turner in St Paul's Cathedral, £20,000 allotted to the Royal Academy, and the remainder divided among the heirs. The 'poor and decayed' artists got nothing, a good example of how the Court of Chancery could defeat a testator's intentions.

A will that proves all of us to be fallible was Lord St Leonards'; he died in 1875, aged ninety-four. His lordship was a former Lord Chancellor, and had been an eminent barrister. He had written a *Handy-book of Property Law*, which adjured all men to make their wills in plenty of time; and he had prepared his own will in spite of saying '... I could, without difficulty, run over the names of many judges and lawyers of note, whose wills, made by themselves, have been set aside or construed so as to defeat every intention they ever had'. He tempted Providence even further: he disapproved of the practice of depositing a will with the Principal Registry of the Court of Probate (Somerset House), saying that a testator could not recover this will easily if he wanted to alter it; and had kept his own will in a box whose key had been kept by his daughter, the Hon Charlotte Sugden, during his last illness.

When Lord St Leonards died, the will could not be found! Fortunately, the Court of Chancery had been abolished (it would have taken ten years at least to disentangle the affair) and the matter came before the Court of Probate. It discovered that during his lifetime, before his last illness, Lord St Leonards had carried the key of the box containing his will and that a duplicate key was locked away in an escritoire. One would have assumed that his lordship would have also carried the key of the escritoire, but it was discovered that there were no less than four keys that would open it. The court never discovered what had happened to the will, but very sensibly accepted what Mrs Sugden could remember of it, and Lord St Leonards' last wishes were carried out. Even experts make mistakes; which is comforting to the rest of us.

The contesting of a will in 1872 led to its being put aside and later to a trial for forgery. The testator was Miss Emma Adolphus; she had in 1866 met a needlewoman called Amelia Clarke who later married a stonemason and became Amelia Jenkins. In 1869 Miss Adolphus took apartments in Leinster Square, Bayswater, London, where her landlady was a Mrs Cooper. Miss Adolphus was in poor health, looking far older than her age, which was in her fifties, and when she died on 4 July 1872 it was found that in her will she had left an annuity of £100 to Mary Cooper, and the residue of her fortune of more than £10,000 to Amelia Jenkins.

The will was contested by her aunt, who charged that the testator was not of sound mind when she had made her will, on account of her illness, but when the case came to court the Solicitor-General stated that the point at issue was whether or not the will had been forged. Deciding this did not take long. Two handwriting experts gave evidence that they had compared the writing of the will with other specimens of Miss Adolphus's handwriting and concluded that they were not the same; at this point the foreman of the jury rose and stated that the jury were convinced that the will had not been written by Miss Adolphus. So the court pronounced the will invalid.

Such a finding could only lead to another trial, for forgery this time. The defendants were Mary Cooper and Amelia Jenkins, and the witnesses to the will, William Hannah and Isaac Hutchinson. The defence was that it was true the will

116

was not strictly in the testator's hand, as Mary Cooper had guided it, but that it did express the testatrix's wishes. The court would have none of this, finding both the women guilty, though acquitting the two witnesses. This acquittal is rather puzzling, because witnesses are supposed to witness the actual signature, and one supposes they did so, or they would not have been acquitted. Therefore, according to the court, the will Miss Adolphus signed in their presence was not a will of whose contents she approved—the two women must have convinced her she was signing a will leaving her money in quite another way. They were sentenced both to seven years' penal servitude, but the jury added a recommendation to mercy, as they had both treated the testator kindly.

It is a well known fact that a criminal cannot benefit in law from the results of his crime—so that if a man murders his wife he cannot inherit under her will. A sad case in 1971 extended this prohibition to manslaughter under certain circumstances. A second wife had murdered her stepson and had been committed to Broadmoor, as she was considered not fit to plead, but was later released into the custody of her husband. In September 1968 she struck her husband on the head and he died a few weeks later, unexpectedly, for which act she was proved guilty of manslaughter and returned to Broadmoor. The argument was whether, under the Homicide Act 1957, she was entitled to inherit under her husband's will when she was not strictly 'morally culpable' of committing a crime, and that Broadmoor anyway was a remedial institution, not a prison. This presented the court with a problem. The judge was sympathetic to the unfortunate woman, but felt that there might be other cases of an entirely different character where diminished responsibility might be pleaded, and the principle that no benefit should accrue for one's crime should be maintained—and so the will was set aside.

NINE

LITERARY WILLS

The chapter title is intended to cover both the wills of writers and the wills they have introduced into their works. Virgil, who died in 10 BC, wanted his *Aeneid* to be burnt after his death, and puts this request in his will. Thousands of school-boys would have been only too pleased about this, but his friends, two of whom were probably his executors Varius and Tucca, persuaded him to change his mind. Like many other Romans, Virgil took the precaution of leaving a quarter of his property to the Emperor Augustus, a necessary step if he was to make sure that the rest of his property was distributed as he wished.

Petrarch, who died in 1374 in Arquà in Italy, remembered another writer in his will and left Boccaccio 200 gold florins to buy a winter robe that would keep him warm during his long hours of study. Erasmus, who died in 1536, ends his will as follows:

Such is my last will, written in my own hand, and sealed with my private seal belonging to my ring, and representing the god Terminus.

William Shakespeare inserted into his will the most famous of all bequests: 'Item: I give unto my wife my second best bed, with the furniture'. This bald statement has led many to sympathise with poor Anne Hathaway; but wives often get

118

scanty mention in wills of the period and earlier, since their interests were generally so well covered by their dower that in wills they often only appear to receive trinkets, jewels or plate, etc. Perhaps the second best bed was more comfortable, perhaps it was the one they used, perhaps it was a private joke between them. We shall never know.

Wills play important parts in several of Shakespeare's plays. Mark Antony rouses the Romans against Caesar's assassins in *Julius Caesar* by producing his will.

> ANTONY: Here is the will and under Caesar's seal.
>   To every Roman citizen he gives,
>   To every several man, seventy five drachmas.
> SECOND CITIZEN: Most noble Caesar! We'll revenge
>   his death.
> THIRD CITIZEN: O royal Caesar!
> ANTONY: Hear me with patience.
> ALL: Peace, ho!
> ANTONY: Moreover, he hath left you all his walks,
>   His private arbours and new planned orchards,
>   On this side Tiber; he hath left them you,
>   And to your heirs for ever, common pleasures,
>   To walk abroad, and recreate yourselves.
>   Here was a Caesar! when comes such another!
> FIRST CITIZEN: Never, never. Come, away, away!
>   We'll burn his body in the holy place,
>   And with the brands fire the traitors' houses.

Shakespeare took the story from Plutarch, who records that Antony did succeed in inflaming the Romans against Caesar's murderers but without mentioning his will, and laughed when Octavius Caesar, Julius Caesar's heir, suggested they paid the citizens their legacies of seventy-five drachmas each.

Another famous will appears in *The Merchant of Venice*, the will of Portia's father, who ordains that Portia shall marry the suitor choosing correctly among the lead, silver and gold caskets:

PORTIA: ... I may neither choose who I would nor refuse who I dislike; so is the will of a living daughter curbed by the will of a dead father. Is it not hard, Nerissa, that I cannot choose one nor refuse none?

NERISSA: Your father was ever virtuous; and holy men at their death have good inspirations; therefore the lottery, that he hath devised in these three chests of gold, silver and lead, whereof who chooses his meaning chooses you ...

Despite Nerissa's defence of Portia's father, in real life he would certainly have consigned Portia to the guardianship of a faithful friend, or, more likely, she would have become a ward of the Doge of Venice. But the chests of gold, silver and lead are more fun, and Portia's lover chooses the right casket with a little help.

Finally, the plight of Orlando in *As You Like It* illustrates the folly of a testator relying on his heir to perform what he should have done himself. Orlando has been left by his father to the care of his elder brother Oliver, who is jealous of him. They quarrel and Orlando takes Oliver by the throat:

OLIVER: Let me go, I say.

ORLANDO: I will not, till I please: you shall hear me. My father charged you in his will to give me good education: you have trained me like a peasant, obscuring and hiding from me all gentleman-like qualities. The spirit of my father grows strong in me, and I will no longer endure it: therefore allow me such exercises as may become a gentleman, or give me the poor allottry my father gave me by testament; with that I will go buy my fortunes.

But Oliver has no intention of giving Orlando his bequest, and the latter finds himself in much the same predicament as the Dashwoods in *Sense and Sensibility* (see p 1).

As expected, the logical French can take a pretty cool look at death. Here is a quote from Montaigne: 'Because mention is made of Death in men's wills and testaments, I warrant you there is none will set his hand to them, till the physician hath given his last doom, and utterly forsaken him'. And Rabelais, who died in 1553, wrote: 'I have no available property, I owe a great deal; the rest I leave to the poor'. He appeared to look on his approaching death as an adventure, for he is reported to have told a messenger from the Cardinal du Bellay who had come to inquire after his health: 'Je vais chercher un grand peût-etre; tirez le rideau, la farce est jouée' ('I am going in search of a great perhaps; lower the curtain, the comedy is over'). *Sang-froid,* 'keeping one's cool', is a quality most of us admire.

Not so cool was John Donne, poet and dean of St Paul's Cathedral, who died in 1631. He made his will '. . . in the fear of God, whose mercy I humbly beg and constantly rely upon in Jesus Christ, and in perfect love and charity with all the world, whose pardon I ask from the lowest of my servants to the highest of my superiors. . . .' He left £500, whose interest was to be applied 'for the maintenance of my dearly beloved mother, whom it hath pleased God after a plentiful fortune in her former times to bring in decay in her very old age'. He also wrote a poem entitled 'The Will':

> Before I sigh my last gasp, let me breathe,
> Great Love, some legacies; I here bequeathe
>   Mine eyes to Argus, if mine eyes can see;
> If they be blind, then Love, I give them thee,
> My tongue to Fame; to ambassadors mine ears;
> To women or the sea my tears;
> Thou, Love, has taught me heretofore
>   By making me serve her who had twenty more,
>   That I should give to none, but such as had too
>   much before.
>
> My constancy I to the planets give;
>   My truth to them who at the court do live;
> Mine ingenuity and openness
>   To Jesuits; to buffoons my pensiveness;
> My silence to any who abroad have been;

My money to a Capuchin:
Thou, Love, taught'st me, by appointing me
To love there, where no love received can be,
Only to give to such as have an incapacity.

This bitter-sweet poem is in great contrast to the simple
emotion felt by the retainers when Sir Roger de Coverly,
Joseph Addison's country squire, makes his will. In the words
of his butler, Edward Biscuit:

It being a very cold day when he made his will, he left for
mourning to every man in the parish a great frize coat, and to
every woman a black riding-hood. It was a most moving sight
to see him take leave of his poor servants, commending us all
for our fidelity, whilst we were not able to speak a word for
weeping. As we most of us are grown grey-headed in our dear
master's service, he has left us pensions and legacies, which
we may live very comfortably upon the remaining part of our
days.

Another eighteenth-century writer, the Rev George Crabbe,
wrote a very moral poem called 'The Will', in which a father
who has an unworthy son wishes to leave his estate to a friend.
But the friend dissuades him, keeping the first will, however,
in case the father should ever wish to revive it:

The will in hand, the Father musing stood.
Then gravely answered, 'Your advice is good;
Yet take the paper and in safety keep;
I'll make another will before I sleep,
But if I hear of some atrocious deed,
That deed I'll burn, and yours will then succeed.
Two thousand I'll bequeath you. No reproof!
And there are some small bequests—he'll have enough;
For if he wastes, he would with all be poor,
And if he wastes not, he will need no more.

The father eventually dies, and

Unhappy Youth! e'er yet the tomb was closed,
And dust to dust conveyed in peace reposed,
He sought his father's closet, searched around,

To find a will: the important will was found.
Well pleased he read, These Lands, this manor, all
Now call me master! I obey the call!
Then from the window looked the valley o'er,
And never saw it look so rich before.
He viewed the dairy, viewed the men at plough,
With other eyes, with other feelings now,
And with a new-formed taste found beauty in a cow.
The distant swain who drove the plough along
Was a good useful slave, and passing strong!
In short, the view was pleasing, nay, was fine,
'Good as my father's, excellent as mine!'
Again he reads,—but he has read enough;
What followed put his virtue to a proof.
'How's this?' to David Wright two thousand pounds!
A monstrous sum! beyond all reason!—zounds!
This is your friendship running out of bounds.
Then here are cousins, Susan, Robert, Joe,
Five hundred each. Do they deserve it? No!
Claim they have none—I wonder if they know
What the good man intended to bestow!
This might be paid—but Wright's enormous sum
Is—I'm alone—there's nobody can come—
'Tis all his hand, no lawyer was employed
To write this prose, that ought to be destroyed!
To no attorney would my father trust:
He wished his son to judge of what was just,
As if he said, My boy will find the will,
And, as he likes, destroy it or fulfil.
This now is reason, this I understand—
What was at his, is now at my command.
As for this paper, with these cousiny names,
I—'tis my Will—commit it to the flames.
Hence! disappear! now I am lord alone:
They'll groan, I know, but, curse them, let them groan!

Then the friend, David Wright, asks if there was a will, not
sure whether the father had fulfilled his promise to write one
out. The son swears there is none, which is his undoing, as
Wright produces his own will and the son loses all. Thus are

the wicked confounded. But not always, for innumerable wills must have been destroyed by heirs unwilling to pay legacies —George II, for instance.

Alexander Pope, who died in 1744, begins his will, 'I, Alexander Pope, of Twickenham in the County of Middlesex, make this my last will and testament. I resign my soul to its Creator in all humble hope of its future happiness as in the disposal of a Being infinitely good'. He also wrote an amusing little poem about a miser about to give up the ghost:

> 'I give and devise' (Old Euchios said,
> And sighed), 'my lands and tenements to Ned'.
> 'Your money, sir?' 'My money, sir, what, all?
> Why,—if I must' (then wept) 'I give it Paul'.
> 'The manor, sir?'—'The manor! hold', he cried,
> 'Not that,—I cannot part with that'—and died.

Pope was, in addition, the anonymous author of a pamphlet, containing a spoof will, published in 1716 and entitled *A Full and True Account of a Horrid and Barbarous Revenge by Poison on the Body of Mr. Edmund Curll, Bookseller. With a faithful Copy of his Last Will and Testament. Published by an Eye Witness.*

In the rough and ready days of the early eighteenth century booksellers and publishers were one and the same, and Curll in fact also sold patent medicines. There were no effective copyright or libel laws, and authors and publishers lifted each other's work at will. Edmund Curll (1675-1747) was always at odds with Pope. He pirated works and libelled the people of the day with the best of them. He published a great number of immoral books, and also a number of excellent books; the former once brought him into the pillory and once on his knees before the bar of the House of Lords.

The title page of Pope's pamphlet, which sold for 3d, contains the following verse:

> So when Curll's stomach the strong Drench o'ercame,
> (Infused in Vengeance of insulted Fame)

The Avenger sees, with a delighted Eye,
His long jaws open, and his Colour fly;
And while his Guts the keen Emeticks urge,
Smiles on the vomit, and enjoys the Purge.

No punches, therefore, are to be pulled from the start. The
text begins:

History furnishes us with Examples of Many Satyrical Authors who have fallen Sacrifices to Revenge, but not of any
Booksellers that I know of, except the unfortunate subject of
the following Papers; I mean Mr Edmund Curll, at the Bible
and Dial in Fleetstreet, who was yesterday Poisoned by Mr.
Pope, after having liv'd many Years an Instance of the Mild
Temper of the British Nation.

The pamphlet goes on to say that Curll had just published
a 'Satyrical Piece' called *Court Poems*, attributed to a Lady of
Quality, Pope and Gay, 'by which indiscreet Method, though
he had escaped one Revenge, there were still two behind in
Reserve'. On the following Wednesday, the pamphlet continues, Mr Lintott, another bookseller, wanted to confer with
Curll, and took him to an inn, The Swan in Fleet Street, for a
'Whet together'. Pope, whose *Homer* Lintott had published,
went with him.

At the inn Pope remonstrates with Curll for wrongfully
attributing poems to him that were not his, and Curll blames
this on another. Pope is apparently reconciled and drinks a
glass of sack to Curll, who responds, 'yet it was plain by the
Pangs this unhappy Stationer felt soon after, that some
poisonous Drug had been secretly induced therein'.

Curll staggers home, where his wife thinks he is bewitched,
but he tells her he suspects Pope. Lintott goes to see him, but
is little use, telling Curll he should have stuck to old hock. He
recommends warm water, but 'Mr Curll did with great
Obstinacy refuse it; which made Mr Lintott infer that he
chose to die, as thinking to recover greater Damages'. Curll
indeed feels he is dying, and asks Lintott to call his partner,

Mr Pemberton, as he feels he should settle his affairs. When Lintott returns with Pemberton, Curll immediately proceeds 'to make a verbal will (Mrs Curll having first put on his Night Cap) in the following manner':

> Gentlemen, in the first Place, I do sincerely pray Forgiveness for those indirect Methods I have pursued in inventing new Titles to old Books, putting Authors Names to Things they never saw, publishing private Quarrels for publick Entertainment; all which I hope will be pardoned, as being done to get an honest livelihood.

He then apologises to those people he has abused, vilified or libelled. He mentions numerous books he has published, the most scurrilous having made him the most profit:

> Dear Mr Pemberton, I beg you to beware of the Indictment at Hick's-Hall for publishing Rochester's bawdy Poems, that Copy will, otherwise be my best Legacy to my dear Wife, and helpless Child.

His family and friends remain by his bedside expecting his death, but then he is relieved by passing 'a plentiful foetid Stool, which obliged them all to retire out of the room'. The pamphleteer does not think he is likely to last more than a month, however, and the pamphlet ends:

> It is to be hoped the other Enemies of this wretched Stationer, will not further pursue their revenge, or shorten this small Period of his miserable Life.

The pamphlet is extremely witty and bitingly satirical. Pope did meet Curll (the only time they ever met) at the Swan, and Curll was given something odd to drink, probably as a practical joke.

No man's will is more consistent with the life he lived than Dr Samuel Johnson's. He died in 1784, like most of us afraid of death, and put off making his will until the last minute. But, having lived a good life, the Doctor 'made a good end', and his will exemplifies his kindness and generosity.

In the Name of God Amen. I Samuel Johnson Esq. in the full possession of my faculties but fearing this night may put an end to my life so ordain this my last will and testament. I bequeath to God a soul polluted with many sins, but I hope purified by repentance and I trust redeemed by Jesus Christ. I leave seven hundred and fifty pounds in the hands of Bennet Langton Esq, three hundred pounds in the hands of Mr Barclay and Mr Perkins Brewers, one hundred and fifty pounds in the hands of Dr. Percy, Bishop of Dromore, ten hundred pounds three per cent annuities in the public funds and one hundred pounds now lying by me in ready money all these beforementioned sums and property I leave I say to Sir Joshua Reynolds, Sir John Hawkins and Doctor William Scott of Doctors Commons in trust for the following uses, that is to say to pay the representatives of the late William Innys Bookseller in St Paul's Churchyard the sum of two hundred pounds. To Mrs White my female servant one hundred pounds stock in the three per cent annuities aforesaid. The rest of the aforesaid sums of Money and Property together with my Books, Plate and household furniture I leave to the before mentioned Sir Joshua Reynolds, Sir John Hawkins and Dr William Scott also in trust to be applied after paying my debts to the use of Francis Barber my man servant, a negro, in such manner as they shall judge most fit and available to his benefit.

On the next day Dr Johnson added a much longer codicil:

By way of Codicil to my last Will and Testament I Samuel Johnson give, devise and bequeath my messuage or tenement situate in Lichfield in the County of Stafford with the appurtenances in the tenure or occupation of Mrs Bond of Lichfield aforesaid or of Mr. Hinchman, her under tenant, to my Executors in trust to sell and dispose of the same, and the money arising from such sale I give and bequeath as follows viz to Thomas and Benjamin the sons of Fisher Johnson late of Leicester and — Whiting, daughter of Thomas Johnson late of Coventry and the grand daughter of the said Thomas Johnson one full and equal fourth part each... I give and bequeath to the Reverend Mr Rogers of Berkley near Froome in the County of Somerset the sum of one hundred pounds requesting him to apply the same towards the maintenance of Elizabeth Herne, a Lunatick. I also give and bequeath to my God children the son and daughter of Mauritius Low, painter, each of them one hundred pounds of my stock in the three per cent consolidated annuities to be applied and disposed of by and at the discretion of my Executors in the Education or Settlement in the world of them my said legatees. Also I give and bequeath to Sir John Hawkins, one of my Executors, the Annales Ecclesiastici of Baronius and Hollinshed's and Stowe's Chronicles and also an octavo Common Prayer Book. To Bennet Langton Esq I give and bequeath my Polyglot Bible. To Sir Joshua Reynolds my Great French Dictionary by Martiniere and my own copy of my folio English Dictionary of the last revision. To Dr William Scott, one of my executors, the Dictionnaire de Commerce and Lectius's Edition of the Greek poets. To Mr Windham Poetae Graeci Heroici per Henricum Stephanum. To the Reverend Mr Strahan, vicar of Islington in Middlesex, Mill's Greek Testament, Beza's Greek Testament by Stephens, all my Latin Bibles and my Greek Bible by Wechelius ... whereas the said Bennet Langton hath agreed in consideration of the sum of seven hundred and fifty pounds mentioned in my Will to be in his hands to grant and secure an annuity of seventy pounds payable during the life of me and my servant Francis Barber and the life of the Survivor of us to Mr George Stubbs in trust for us my mind and will is that in case of my decease before the said agreement shall be perfected the said sum of seven hundred and fifty pounds and the Bond for securing the said sum shall go to the said Francis Barber and I hereby give and bequeath to him the same in lieu of the bequest in his favour, contained in my said will and I hereby empower my Executors to deduct and retain all expenses that shall or may be incurred in the execution of my said will and of this codicil thereto out of such estate and Effects as I shall die possessed of. All the Rest, Residue and Remainder of my Estate and Effects I give and bequeath to my said Executors in trust for Mr Francis Barber, his Executors and Administrators. Witness my hand and seal this ninth day of December 1784—Sam: Johnson.

The main legatee, Francis Barber, was a negro from Jamaica

who had been brought to England in 1750 by Colonel Bathurst, father of Johnson's friend Dr Bathurst. The Colonel gave him his freedom in his will and he entered Johnson's service in March 1752, just after the death of Johnson's wife Tetty. They were great friends, and Barber remained with Johnson till his master's death in 1784, apart from two interruptions: once when he went to work for an apothecary in Cheapside, though still visiting his master occasionally; and, the second time, when he left Johnson's employ about 1759 to join the navy. Such an action is astonishing in a century when most navy men were press-ganged; Barber appears to have joined freely, and Johnson evidently thought the lad's decision foolish, for he loathed the sea himself and thought any man would be better off in jail. It was an age of patronage, so he wrote to Tobias Smollett, asking him to use his good offices with John Wilkes to free Barber from his servitude, which, however, Barber was quite happy to endure. Smollett wrote to Wilkes on 16 March 1759, his letter a model for anyone asking a favour:

Dear Sir,
    I am again your petitioner on behalf of that great Cham of literature, Samuel Johnson. His black servant, whose name is Francis Barber, has been pressed on board the Stag Frigate, Captain Angel, and our lexicographer is in great distress. He says, the boy is a sickly lad, of a delicate frame, and particularly subject to a malady in his throat, which renders him very unfit for his Majesty's service. You know what matter of animosity the said Johnson has against you: and I dare say you desire no other opportunity of resenting it, than that of laying him under an obligation. He was humble enough to desire my assistance on this occasion, though he and I were never cater-cousins; and I gave him to understand that I would make application to my friend Mr. Wilkes, who, perhaps, by his interest with Dr. Hay and Mr. Elliot, might be able to procure the discharge of his lacquey. It would be superfluous to say more on the subject, which I leave to your own considera-

129

tion; but I cannot let slip this opportunity of declaring that I am, with the most inviolable esteem and attachment, dear Sir,
Your affectionate,
obliged humble servant.
T Smollett

Wilkes duly applied to his friend Sir George Hay, who was one of the Lords Commissioners of the Admiralty, and Barber was returned to his master.

Both Colonel Bathurst and Johnson had taken great pains with Barber's education, the former sending him to school at the Rev Mr Jackson's at Barton in Yorkshire, and Johnson, to schools in Northamptonshire and at Bishop Stortford, Herts. Johnson's bequest was worth about £1,500 to Barber, and, after his master's death, he and his wife went to live in Lichfield, Dr Johnson's birthplace, where he died in 1801 in Stafford Infirmary after a painful illness.

Johnson's bequest to his faithful servant was natural, as he had no close relations. His kindness is also shown in his bequest of £100 for the support of 'Elizabeth Herne a Lunatick' in an age when lunacy was more a subject for mirth than consideration.

His library was sold after his death for almost £250, though it was not large. Many people, however, wished to have a remembrance of the good doctor. It is interesting to note that Dr Johnson had invested £300 in Barclay & Perkins, the brewers, who have apparently never advertised the fact.

Jane Austen was born in the eighteenth century, and in spirit her novels belong to it. In *Sense and Sensibility*, published in 1811, the Dashwoods—Mrs Dashwood and three daughters—are poor compared with their half-brother, Mrs Dashwood's stepson, who has been recommended by their father on his deathbed to do something for his half-sisters. His father cannot will them any more than he has, because the estate he inherited is to pass to his son under a previous will.

The stepson at first considers giving the girls £1,000 pounds each: 'Yes, he would give them three thousand pounds; it would be liberal and handsome! ... he could spare so considerable a sum with little inconvenience'.

But after a conversation with his wife the sum is first reduced to £500 each, and then, after some further thought, an annuity of £100 a year for the mother is decided upon, but—

His wife hesitated a little, however, in giving her consent to this plan.

'To be sure', said she, 'it is better than parting with fifteen hundred pounds at once. But then, if Mrs Dashwood should live fifteen years, we shall be completely taken in'.

'Fifteen years! my dear Fanny; her life cannot be worth half that purchase.'

'Certainly not; but if you observe, people always live for ever when there is any annuity to be paid them ...'

So the annuity is argued away, and the stepson finally decides that a 'present of fifty pounds now and then will prevent their ever being distressed for money, and will, I think, be amply discharging my promise to my father'. What began as an intention to give £3,000 to his half-sisters has now dwindled to an occasional present of £50. From this sum it is a short step to giving them nothing apart from presents of fish and game when they are in season, and 'he finally resolved that it would be absolutely unnecessary, if not highly indecorous, to do more for the widow and children of his father than such kind of neighbourly acts as his own wife pointed out'. Jane Austen's story again exemplifies the rule that a testator who wishes to get something done must do it himself.

There was a superstition dating from the sixteenth century at the latest and still prevalent, if unconsciously so, that if you make your will you are about to die. Many of us leave will-making until the last moment, and it is probably for this very reason. Charles Lamb recognised this fear when he wrote, 'I want to make my will and leave my property in trust for my sister. N.B. I am not *therefore* going to die'.

His contemporary, William Wordsworth (1770-1850), was lucky enough to receive a legacy of £900 from a friend, Raisley Calvert, in 1795, which relieved him of the necessity of making a living and allowed him to write poetry. Wordsworth wrote rather a stiff poem of thanks, perhaps illustrating that such thanks come much better in prose:

> A youth—(he bore
> The name of Calvert—it shall live, if words
> Of mine can give it life), in firm belief
> That by endowments not from one withheld
> Good might be furthered—in his last decay
> By a bequest sufficient for my needs
> Enabled me to pause for choice, and walk
> At large and unrestrained, nor damped too soon
> By mortal cares. Himself no poet, yet
> Far less a common follower of the world,
> He dreamed that my pursuits and labours lay
> Apart from all that leads to wealth, or even
> A necessary maintenance insures,
> Without some hazard of the finer sense;
> He cleaved a passage for me, and the stream
> Flowed in the bent of nature.

Dickens was a great man for wills, and a great man for exploding the Court of Chancery, as readers of *Bleak House* will know. Dickens' prize specimen is Mr Spenlow, to whom David Copperfield is articled and whose daughter, Dora, he loves. Mr Spenlow learns of their attachment through the interference of David's *bete noire*, Miss Murdstone, and is very cold towards the idea, implying that an upstart like David should not have the impertinence to aspire to the hand of a rich lawyer's daughter. He gives David the impression that she will receive a large fortune at his death and that all his affairs are in perfect trim:

'And you can hardly think', said Mr. Spenlow, 'having experience of what we see, in the Commons here, every day, of the various unaccountable and negligent proceedings of men, in respect of their testamentary arrangements—of all subjects, the one on which perhaps the strangest revelations of human inconsistency are to be met with—but that mine are made?'

David is impressed. Later, Mr Spenlow dies suddenly. His partner, Jorkins, and old Tiffey, the clerk, call David into the office to help them.

'Oh!' said Mr. Jorkins. 'Mr. Tiffey and myself, Mr. Copperfield, are about to examine the desks, the drawers, and other such repositories of the deceased, with a view of sealing up his private papers, and searching for a will. There is no trace of any, elsewhere. It may be as well for you to assist us if you please'.

They search unsuccessfully for some time until Mr Jorkins observes that he is disposed to think that Mr Spenlow died without making a will. But David knows better:

'Oh, I know he had!' I said.
They both stopped and looked at me.
'On the very day when I last saw him,' said I, 'he told me that he had, and that his affairs were long since settled.'
Mr. Jorkins and old Tiffey shook their heads with one accord.
'That looks unpromising,' said Tiffey.
'Very unpromising,' said Mr Jorkins.
'Surely you don't doubt—' I began.
'My good Mr. Copperfield!' said Tiffey, laying his hand upon my arm, and shutting up both his eyes as he shook his head; 'if you had been in the Commons as long as I have, you would know that there is no subject on which men are so inconsistent, and so little to be trusted.'
'Why, bless my soul, he made that very remark!' I replied persistently.
'I should call that almost final,' observed Tiffey. 'My opinion is—no will.'
It appeared a wonderful thing to me, but it turned out that there *was* no will. He had never so much as thought of making one . . .

Mr Spenlow, from fiction, is not so far removed from Lord St Leonards, in real life. Wills have, indeed, been found in strange places. Tony Weller, in Dickens' *Pickwick Papers*, found his wife's will in a teapot:

> 'Samivel,' said Mr. Weller, accosting his son on the morning after the funeral, 'I've found it, Sammy. I thought it wos there.'
>
> 'Thought wot wos were?' inquired Sam.
>
> 'Your mother-in-law's vill, Sammy,' replied Mr. Weller. 'In wirtue o' vich, them arrangements is to be made as I told you on, last night, respectin' the funs.'
>
> 'Wot, didn't she tell you were it wos?' inquired Sam.
>
> 'Not a bit on it, Sammy,' replied Mr. Weller. 'We wos a adjestin' our little differences, and I wos a cheerin' her spirits and bearin' her up, so that I forgot to ask anythin' about it. I don't know as I should ha' done it indeed, if I had remembered it,' added Mr. Weller, 'for it's a rum sort o' thing, Sammy, to go a hankerin' arter anybody's property, ven you're assistin' 'em in illness. It's like helping an outside passenger up, ven he's been pitched off a coach, and puttin' your hand in his pocket, vile you ask him vith a sigh how he finds hisself, Sammy.'
>
> With this figurative illustration of his meaning, Mr. Weller unclasped his pocket-book, and drew forth a dirty sheet of letter paper, on which were inscribed various characters crowded together in remarkable confusion.
>
> 'This here is the dockyment, Sammy,' said Mr. Weller. 'I found it in the little black teapot, on the top shelf o' the bar closet...'

Mr Weller is a coachman and generally illustrates his views with similes from the world of the stagecoach, and his wife had been landlady of an inn. He had difficulties with his 'ws' and 'vs', but his heart was in the right place. Having told Sam that his wife has left her stepson 'two hundred pounds vurth o' reduced counsels' and the rest to her husband, also making him her executor, Tony is quite prepared to burn the will:

'Wot are you a-doin' on, you lunatic?' said Sam, snatching
the paper away, as his parent, in all innocence, stirred the
fire preparatory to suiting the action to the word. 'You're a
nice eggzekiter, you are.'

'Vy not!' inquired Mr. Weller, looking sternly round, with
the poker in his hand.

'Vy not!' exclaimed Sam. ' 'Cos it must be proved, and probated, and swore to, and all manner o' formalities.'

Sam and Mr Weller, with two coachmen just as fat as the
latter, and a lawyer, Solomon Pell, then lunch together and go
off to Doctors' Commons, where the will is eventually proved
satisfactorily. Another will to be proved in the same place is
Mr Barkis's will in *David Copperfield*. David, training himself
to be a lawyer at the time, goes there with Mr Barkis's widow,
Peggotty, and proves the will successfully. But his opinion of
Doctors' Commons, the principal registry for wills for the
Prerogative Court of Canterbury (a predecessor to Somerset
House), is not high:

> ...I submitted that I thought the Prerogative Office rather a
> queerly managed institution. Mr. Spenlow inquired in what
> respect? I replied, with all due deference to his experience...
> that perhaps it was a little nonsensical that the Registry of
> that Court, containing the original wills of all persons leaving
> effects within the immense province of Canterbury, for three
> whole centuries, should be an accidental building, never de-
> signed for the purpose, leased by the registrars for their own
> private emolument, unsafe, not even ascertained to be fire-
> proof, choked with the important documents it held, and posi-
> tively, from the roof to the basement, a mercenary speculation
> of the registrars, who took great fees from the public, and
> crammed the public's wills away anyhow and anywhere, hav-
> ing no other object than to get rid of them cheaply... That,
> perhaps, it was a little unjust, that all the great offices in this
> great office should be magnificent sinecures, while the unfor-
> tunate working-clerks in the cold dark room up-stairs were the
> worst rewarded, and the least considered men, doing import-
> ant services, in London. That perhaps it was a little indecent

135

that the principal registrar of all, whose duty it was to find the public, constantly resorting to this place, all needful accommodation, should be an enormous sinecurist ... while the public was put to the inconvenience of which we had a specimen every afternoon, when the office was busy, and which we knew to be quite monstrous. That, perhaps, in short, this Prerogative Office of the diocese of Canterbury was altogether such a pestilent job, and such a pernicious absurdity, that but for its being squeezed away in a corner of Saint Paul's Churchyard, which few people knew, it must have been turned completely inside out, and upside down, long ago.

David Copperfield was published in 1849-50, but in 1826 N. H. Nicolas, author of *Testamenta Vetusta*, was equally critical in the preface he wrote to that work, this time of the way Doctors' Commons was run. He found it very difficult to get any information:

... whilst the total absence of every thing like urbanity, even if a stronger expression be not merited, in the deportment of those with whom the public come in collision at the principal Registry in the Kingdom—that at Doctors' Commons—deterred the Editor from soliciting permission to transcribe or collate the wills here abstracted with such of the originals, or recorded copies as exist there.

The person who, when perusing a will in that Repository, has once experienced the rude manner of address to which the applicants are subject, and the still more insolent tone in which it is sometimes uttered, must be endowed with an unusual forbearance if he subjects himself to such conduct when he can possibly avoid it.

Dickens' own will records him as Charles John Huffham Dickens, and, rather plaintively, mentions his wife:

... I desire here simply to record the fact that my wife since our separation by consent has been in the receipt from me of an annual income of six hundred pounds, while all the great charges of a numerous and expensive family have devolved wholly upon myself.

He later adds directions concerning his funeral:

> I emphatically direct that I be buried in an inexpensive,
> unostentatious and strictly private manner, that no public
> announcement be made of the time or place of my burial, that
> at the utmost not more than three plain mourning coaches be
> employed, and that those who attend my funeral wear no scarf,
> cloak, black bow, long hatband or other such revolting absur-
> dity... I require my friends on no account to make me the
> subject of any monument, memorial or testimonial whatever.
> I rest my claims to the remembrance of my Country upon my
> published works, and to the remembrance of my friends upon
> their experience of me in addition.

Dickens died in 1870, leaving under £80,000. Robert
Browning died nineteen years later, in 1889, leaving £16,775.
The contents of his will are commonplace, but the witnesses
to his signature are certainly not—A. Tennyson and F. T.
Palgrave, the Poet Laureate and the famous compiler of the
Golden Treasury. Browning's will was prepared many years
before his death, and one assumes that at one time, when his
two literary friends were staying with him, he used their services as witnesses.

Robert Louis Stevenson's Dr Jekyll was in a quandary concerning his *alter ego* Mr Hyde, but solved it by making Mr
Hyde his legatee, and ordering in his will that if he disappeared
for three months or more Hyde was to inherit. This annoyed
Jekyll's solicitor, who, of course, had never seen Hyde.

Howards End, by E. M. Forster, provides an example of a
will (really a codicil) destroyed by executors. Mrs Wilcox had
owned and loved the house, Howards End, in which she and
her husband lived. Her will left everything to him, but after
her death a note arrives from the nursing home in which she
had died in her handwriting, but in pencil and unsigned, asking that her house should go to Margaret Schlegel, who had
been her friend for a short time. Mr Wilcox, his son Charles
and daughter Evie discuss the matter. They feel betrayed, not

realising or unwilling to accept that Mrs Wilcox had left Howards End to Margaret Schlegel as a person who might come to love the house as she did and in a way her family never could do. Unconsciously, Mrs Wilcox has given them a way out, since the bequest is not included in her will. Perhaps she was too ill to attend to that, but it seems more likely that she was just telling them that she would like the house to go to someone else rather than them, but if they wished they could destroy the note. The family is rich, so there is no question that the worth of the house means anything, but none of them like the Schlegels much. The latter are intellectual Londoners, half German, the Wilcoxes solid no-nonsense English. The Wilcoxes grieve for their mother, but persuade themselves that the note was written because she was ill at the time and not responsible for her actions. The will is torn up. So soon do the wishes of the dead lose their power. Howards End does eventually come to Margaret Schlegel because she marries Mr Wilcox.

George Bernard Shaw, who died in 1950 at the age of 94, left an interesting will:

> I desire that my dead body should be cremated and its ashes inseparately mixed with those of my late wife now in the custody of the Golders Green Crematorium and in this condition inurned or scattered in the garden of the house at Ayot Saint Lawrence where we lived together for thirty five years, unless some other disposal of them should be in the opinion of my Trustee more eligible. Personally I prefer the garden to the cloister.

He went on to say that as his religions convictions could only be defined as 'those of a believer in Creative Evolution', he desired that no method of commemorating him should suggest that he 'accepted the tenets peculiar to any established church or denomination'. He also requested that no memorial should 'take the form of a cross or any other instrument of torture or symbol of blood sacrifice'.

138

After numerous bequests he ends on a note of controversy, as would perhaps be expected of a man who had always been controversial. He leaves a bequest to investigate the time and money that would be saved throughout the English-speaking world by using what he called the Proposed British Alphabet of forty letters instead of the standard alphabet, which he calls Dr Johnson's alphabet. He says that the inquiry must be conducted scientifically, without regard 'to the views of professional and amateur phoneticians, etymologists, Spelling Reformers, patentees of universal languages, inventors of shorthand codes for verbatim reporting or rival alphabets, teachers of the established orthography, disputants about pronunciation, or any of the irreconcilables whose wranglings have overlooked and confused the single issue of labour saving and made change impossible during the last hundred years'.

He also wishes a phonetic expert to prepare the text of his play *Androcles and the Lion* in the Proposed British Alphabet 'assuming the pronunciation to resemble that recorded of His Majesty our late King George V and sometimes described as Northern English'. The king's broadcasts had been celebrated for their clarity and simplicity, and his voice admired greatly during his reign. Once the play had been prepared Shaw wished a 'fair copy' to be made of the text, because there would be no printing type available to reproduce it, the new version printed page by page with the standard alphabet, and copies of the combined edition sent to the major libraries throughout the world. He hoped the Ministry of Education would take up his new alphabet. He speaks about the Proposed British Alphabet as follows:

I leave my Trustee to bear in mind that the Proposed British Alphabet does not pretend to be exhaustive as it contains only sixteen vowels, whereas by infinitesimal movements of the tongue countless different vowels can be produced, all of them in use among speakers of English who utter the same vowels no oftener than they make the same fingerprints. Nevertheless they can understand one another's speech and writing sufficiently to converse or correspond: for instance, a graduate of Trinity College Dublin has no difficulty in understanding a graduate of Oxford University when one says that 'the sun rohze' and the other 'the sun rahoeze', nor are either of them puzzled when a peasant calls his childhood his 'chawldid'. For a university graduate calls my native country Ahlind.

He concludes his will:

... I also record my regret that my means are not sufficient to provide for material pledges of my regard for the many friends, who as colleagues in the Socialistic movement or as artists co-operating with me in the performance of my plays or otherwise have not only made my career possible but hallowed it with kindly human relations.

The Probate Court held that the provisions in Shaw's will concerning the alphabet were impossible to carry out as they stood, and so the money was given to three charities he had designated as a second choice, with a proviso that they should do something towards fulfilling his wishes. Quite a lot was done. A competition was held and the alphabet was chosen; and the play *Androcles and the Lion* was published and distributed.

Finally, to end with that other prophet of the twentieth century, George Orwell, who died in 1950—he requests that he be buried, not cremated, according to Church of England rites in the nearest convenient cemetery, and that his grave be marked plainly with his real name, Eric Arthur Blair, and the dates of his birth and death. He wants no memorial service and no biography written.

SOME ESTATES, 1863-1971

Years of death are given in brackets

Archer, Fred (1886)—Champion jockey £72,286
Arnaud, Yvonne (1958)—Actress £3,550
Arnold, Matthew (1888)—Poet £1,040
Asquith, H. H., Earl of Oxford (1928)—Prime
Minister £9,345
Astor, Nancy, Viscountess (1964)—First woman
MP £25,467
Attlee, Clement, Earl (1967)—Prime Minister £7,295
Austin, Herbert, Baron (1941)—Car manufacturer £509,712
Ayres, Ruby M. (1955)—Novelist £29,327
Baird, John Logie (1946)—TV pioneer £7,370
Baldwin, Stanley, Earl (1947)—Prime Minister £280,971
Bax, Sir Arnold (1953)—Master of the King's
Music £11,936
Beatty, David, Earl (1936)—Commander of battle-
cruiser squadron at Battle of Jutland £174,903
Beaverbrook, Lord (1964)—Newspaper proprietor £379,530
Beecham, Sir Thomas (1961)—Conductor £10,802
Bevin, Ernest (1951)—Foreign Secretary £13,989
Birkett, Norman, Lord (1962)—Barrister and judge £43,295
Blunt, Wilfrid Scawen (1922)—Poet £79,469

Booth, General William (1912)—Founder of
  Salvation Army   £3,160
Bouch, Sir Thomas (1880)—Designer of Tay Bridge
  blown down in 1879   £218,000
Bragg, Sir William (1942)—Scientist, Nobel Prize
  winner   £27,039
Brooke, Rupert (1915)—Poet   £923
Brunel, Isambard Kingdom (1859)—Engineer
      under £90,000
Buller, Sir Redvers (1908)—Soldier, Commander at
  Spion Kop and Relief of Ladysmith   £39,781
Burton, Sir Richard (1890)—Explorer, writer   £188
Cadbury, George (1922)—Quaker philanthropist £1,071,100
Campbell-Bannerman, Sir Henry (1908)—Prime
  Minister   £175,580
Cardigan, 7th Earl of (1868)—Leader of Charge of
  the Light Brigade at Balaclava   under £60,000
Carroll, Lewis (1898)—Writer   £4,596
Chamberlain, Joseph (1914)—Politician   £125,495
Chamberlain, Neville (1940)—Prime Minister   £84,013
Chesterton, G. K. (1936)—Writer   £28,390
Churchill, Lord Randolph (1895)—Politician, father
  of Sir Winston Churchill   £75,971
Churchill, Sir Winston (1965)—Statesman, Prime
  Minister   £304,044
Cripps, Sir Stafford (1952)—Chancellor of the
  Exchequer   £15,191
Cunningham, Andrew, Viscount (1962)—Admiral   £15,311
Cunningham, Sir John (1962)—Admiral   £25,514
Curzon, 1st Marquess (1925)—Viceroy of India   £343,280
Davidson, Randall Thomas (1930)—Archbishop of
  Canterbury   £34,946
Davies, Sir Walford (1941)—Master of the King's
  Music   £3,573

Appendix

Dickens, Charles (1870)—Writer   under £80,000
Disraeli, Benjamin, Earl of Beaconsfield (1881)—
   Prime Minister   £84,020
Donat, Robert (1958)—Actor   £25,237
Du Maurier, Sir Gerald (1934)—Actor   £17,996
Duveen, Joseph, 1st Baron (1939)—Art connoisseur   £2,814
Elgar, Sir Edward (1934)—Composer   £13,934
Eliot, T. S. (1965)—Poet   £105,272
Ellerman, Sir John Reeves (1933)—Shipping
   magnate   £36,684,265
Engels, Friedrich (1895)—Co-founder of
   Communism   £25,265
Ferrier, Kathleen (1952)—Singer   £15,135
Field, Sid (1950)—Comedian   £31,736
Fisher, John, Lord (1920)—Admiral, First Sea Lord £23,809
Fitzgerald, Edward (1883)—Poet, translator of
   Omar Khayyám   £35,773
Fleming, Ian (1964)—Writer, creator of James Bond £302,147
Fleming, Sir Alexander (1955)—Scientist, discoverer
   of penicillin   £29,322
Fowler, H. W. (1933)—Grammarian   £3,270
Fox Talbot, W. H. (1877)—Film pioneer   under £12,000
French, John, Earl of Ypres (1925)—Soldier,
   Commander of BEF in 1914   £20,615
Freud, Sigmund (1939)—Originator of
   psychoanalysis   £22,850
Gibson, Wing-Cdr Guy Penrose (1944)—Leader
   of the Dambusters   £2,925
Gilbert, Sir William S. (1911)—Librettist of the
   Savoy Operas   £118,028
Gladstone, William Ewart (1898)—Prime Minister £58,569
Goddard, Lord (1971)—Lord Chief Justice   £147,696
Gordon, Charles George (1885)—Soldier, killed at
   Khartoum   £2,315

143

Gort, John, Viscount (1946)—Soldier, Commander
  of BEF in 1940   £173,326
Grace, Dr W. G. (1915)—Cricketer   £7,279
Grahame, Kenneth (1932)—Writer   £41,898
Hamilton, Sir Ian (1947)—Soldier, Commander in
  Gallipoli, 1915   £98,056
Handley-Page, Sir Frederick (1962)—Aircraft
  manufacturer   £140,960
Handley, Tommy (1949)—Comedian   £63,182
Hardy, Thomas (1928)—Writer   £95,418
Hay, Will (1949)—Comedian   £27,155
Hill, Sir Rowland (1879)—Originator of penny post
                                        under £60,000
Hobbs, Sir John Berry (1963)—Jack Hobbs, cricketer £19,445
Holst, Gustav (1934)—Composer   £9,318
Howard, Leslie (1943)—Actor   £62,762
Jardine, Douglas (1958)—Cricketer, captain of
  England   £71,274
Jellicoe, John, Earl (1935)—Admiral, Commander at
  Battle of Jutland   £13,363
John, Augustus (1961)—Painter   £90,788
Keynes, John Maynard, Baron (1946)—Economist   £484,864
Kitchener of Khartoum, Earl (1916)—Soldier   £171,422
Korda, Sir Alexander (1956)—Film producer   £385,685
Lansbury, George (1940)—Leader of Labour Party   £1,696
Laski, Harold J. (1950)—Economist   £19,558
Lawrence, D. H. (1930)—Writer   £2,439
Lawrence, T. E. (1935)—Lawrence of Arabia   £7,441
Leverhulme, William, Viscount (1925)—
  Manufacturer, Lever Brothers   £1,625,409
Lipton, Sir Thomas (1931)—Industrialist and
  sportsman   £600,105
Lister, Joseph, Lord (1912)—Surgeon, discoverer of
  antiseptic surgery   £67,996

Lloyd George, David, Earl (1945)—Prime Minister £140,000
MacColl, René (1971)—Journalist   £29,627
Mallory, George (1924)—Mountaineer, lost on Everest £1,708
Marconi, Guglielmo, Marchese (1937)—Radio
  pioneer   £45,529
Martin-Harvey, Sir John (1944)—Actor   £12,738
Marx, Karl (1883)—Founder of Communism   £250
Maxim, Sir Hiram (1916)—Armament inventor   £33,800
Meredith, George (1909)—Novelist   £32,359
Miles, Michael (1971)—TV quizmaster   £85,932
Mill, John Stuart (1873)—Economist   under £14,000
Mills, Bertram W. (1938)—Circus owner   £131,012
Morris, William (1896)—Leader of Arts and Crafts
  Movement   £54,118
Morrison, Herbert, Baron (1965)—Foreign Secretary,
  leader of LCC   £28,600
Murry, John Middleton (1957)—Writer   £31,758
Nightingale, Florence (1910)—Founder of modern
  nursing   £36,128
Northcliffe, Alfred Harmsworth, Lord (1922)—
  Newspaper proprietor   £5,248,973
Nuffield, Lord (1963)—Car manufacturer,
  philanthropist   £3,250,000
Oman, Sir Charles (1946)—Historian   £42,760
Orwell, George (1950)—Writer   £9,909
Pankhurst, Mrs Emmeline (1920)—Suffragette   £86
Plimsoll, Samuel (1898)—Originator of Plimsoll Line £40,849
Pollitt, Harry (1960)—Leader of British Communist
  Party   £1,169
Pound, Sir Dudley (1943)—Admiral, First Sea Lord   £1,964
Roberts, Frederick Sleigh, Earl (1914)—Soldier   £77,304
Robertson, Sir William (1933)—Soldier, CIGS in
  World War I   £50,118
Rolls, Hon C. S. (1910)—Car manufacturer   £30,936

Rowntree, Joseph (1925)—Quaker philanthropist £220,336
Royce, Henry (1933)—Car manufacturer £110,202
Ruskin, John (1900)—Writer, critic £10,660
Rutherford, Ernest, Baron (1937)—Scientist,
 Nobel Prize winner £7,402
Sargent, J. S. (1925)—Painter £25,794
Sayers, Dorothy (1957)—Writer £36,279
Segrave, Sir Henry (1930)—Racing driver £18,795
Sewell, Anna (1878)—Author of *Black Beauty* under £2,000
Shaftesbury, 7th Earl of (1885)—Social reformer £32,352
Sitwell, Dame Edith (1964)—Poet £28,836
Snowdon, Philip, Viscount (1937)—Chancellor of the
 Exchequer £3,367
Speke, John Hanning (1864)—Explorer, discoverer of
 the source of the Nile under £2,000
Spencer, Sir Stanley (1959)—Painter £8,449
Stanley, Sir Henry Morton (1904)—Explorer £145,866
Strachey, Lytton (1932)—Writer £9,655
Sullivan, Sir Arthur (1900)—Composer of the
 Savoy Operas £56,537
Swift, Frank (1958)—Footballer, England's goalkeeper £3,592
Tauber, Richard (1948)—Singer £2,472
Temple, William (1944)—Archbishop of Canterbury £28,549
Tennyson, Alfred, Lord (1892)—Poet Laureate £57,207
Thackeray, William Makepeace (1863)—Writer
 under £20,000
Terry, Ellen (1928)—Actress £22,231
Tree, Sir Herbert Beerbohm (1917)—Actor-manager £44,086
Trenchard, Hugh, Viscount (1956)—Airman and
 Commissioner of Police £3,577
Waugh, Evelyn (1960)—Writer £20,068
Wavell, Archibald, Earl (1950)—Soldier £49,580
Wells, H. G. (1946)—Writer £59,811
Whitten-Brown, Sir Arthur (1948)—Airman, first

to fly Atlantic nonstop	£5,002
Whymper, Edward (1911)—Mountaineer, first to climb Matterhorn	£5,525
Winn, Godfrey (1971)—Writer	£361,601
Wood, Sir Henry (1944)—Conductor, founder of Promenade Concerts	£6,460
Woolf, Virginia (1941)—Writer	£14,051

BIBLIOGRAPHY AND ACKNOWLEDGEMENTS

Much of my information has come from the following books, whose authors I should thank, if it were possible:

Byrne, Mrs J. C. *Curiosities of the Search Room* (1880)

Hall, E. Vine. *The Romance of Wills and Testaments* (1912)

Harris, V. M. *Ancient, Curious and Famous Wills* (1911)

Nicolas, N. H. *Testamenta Vetusta* (1826)

Nichols, J. G. & Bruce, John. *Wills from Doctors Commons* (1863)

Nichols, John. *Royal Wills* (1780)

Sharpe, R. R. *Calendar of Wills proved and enrolled in the Court of Husting, London* (1889-90)

I thank the Librarian of the Law Society for putting me on the track of wills, and others who have answered specific questions. I am grateful to the Ford Foundation, the Carnegie Corporation, the Rockefeller Foundation, Rockefeller Family and Associates, and the Nuffield Foundation for reports and much information in other forms. I also thank E. R. Delderfield for allowing me to use a will that appears in his *Book of True Animal Stories*; the Archivist for Presidential Libraries, Washington DC, for useful information; John F. Albano, Chief Clerk of the Surrogate's Court of the County of Dutchess, Poughkeepsie NY, for details of President Franklin D. Roosevelt's will; and my brother Peter for preparing much of the Appendix.

INDEX

Index